The Dominican friary church at Gloucester, later altered into a house

MEDIEVAL ENGLISH FRIARIES

Mike Salter

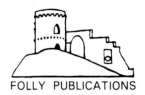

FOLLY PUBLICATIONS

ACKNOWLEDGEMENTS

The photographs in this book were taken by the author, most of them during 2009, although a few go back to the 1980s. The author also drew the map inside the front cover and all the plans. Thanks for various services are due to Richard Carlton, Jean Cuddeford, Anne Ling and Peter Ryder, and also to Paul and Allan at Aspect Design for help with the cover artwork.

ABOUT THIS BOOK

This book is a sequel to the recent volume Abbeys and Friaries of Ireland in which plans of many Irish friaries are shown on a scale of 1:400. This is the scale used for two thirds of the plans in this book, and also almost all the plans in the parish churches books of this series. This allows some interesting comparisions. The same system of cross-hatching is also used to denote work of different centuries. Note that some things are difficult to convey on small scale plans and in some cases walling is shown as being of a specific century when it is in fact difficult to date with any certainty. The buildings were measured by the author in metres and only metric scales are given. Three metres almost equals ten feet for those still wanting imperial measures.

Grid references of two letters and six figures are given in the gazetteers to allow standing remains to be pin-pointed on the O.S. 1:50,000 scale Landranger maps. Less than half of the friaries can be accurately located by standing remains or parts once revealed by excavations so the exact location of some of the houses remains in doubt.

The main focus is on the medieval development and usage of each site. Lack of space in a book intended to be reasonably compact and inexpensive prohibits more than brief comments about subsequent usage of any of the sites, nor can much be said about later or modern features and furnishings within the few buildings that are still in use. For similar reasons only brief details are given of the results of excavations, concentrating mainly on walls and floors found rather than lengthy discussions about any artifacts brought to the surface. For those friaries for which a wealth of information survives about the friars and their benefactors and their relationships with the secular and ecclesiastical authorities (notably those at Cambridge, Canterbury, Lincoln, Northampton, Oxford, Scarborough, Worcester and York) only a selection of the most important events and people involved has been included in the gazetteer.

ABOUT THE AUTHOR

Mike Salter is 56 and has been a professional author and publisher since 1988. He is particularly interested in the planning and layout of medieval buildings and has a huge collection of plans of abbeys, churches and castles he has measured during tours (mostly by bicycle and public transport) throughout all parts of the British Isles since 1968. Wolverhampton born and bred, Mike now lives in an old cottage beside the Malvern Hills. His other interests include walking, geocaching, maps, railways, board games, morris dancing and playing percussion instruments and calling English folk dances occasionally with local folk groups.

First published March 2010. Copyright Mike Salter 2010.
Reprinted July 2010 incorporating a number of alterations mostly resulting from some correspondence with Peter Ryder, to whom special thanks are due.
Folly Publications, Folly Cottage, 151 West Malvern Rd, Malvern, Worcs WR14 4AY
Printed by Aspect Design, 89 Newtown Rd, Malvern, Worcestershire WR14 2PD

The cloister at Aylesford Carmetite Friary

CONTENTS

A map of the friaries appears inside the back of the cover

INTRODUCTION TO THE FRIARS

The friars of the order founded by St Dominic in 1216 were the first mendicant friars to arrive in England. Noted as preachers and for encouraging study and education, they followed the rule of St Augustine as established by 11th century reformers from the writings of St Augustine of Hippo, and were known as the Black Friars from the colour of the cloaks they wore over white habits. In 1221 thirteen of them under Prior Gilbert de Fresnoy came over from France with Peter des Roches, Bishop of Winchester. They were made welcome after Prior Gilbert greatly impressed Archbishop Stephen Langton with his preaching. The order soon established itself in many towns, having about fifty English houses organised in four divisions each overseen by a head house.

Next to arrive in England were the Franciscans or Grey Friars, nine of whom landed at Dover in 1224, the same year that their founder, St Francis of Assisi, first displayed on his body the stigmata, or signs of the Five Wounds of Christ. They followed a simple rule devised by St Francis from sayings in the Gospels and were preachers who lived a life of absolute poverty, originally owning literally nothing, following the example of St Francis after his call to cast off his worldly life and preach in 1208. Substantial parts still remain of a quarter of their English houses, which numbered nearly sixty.

Bishop Peter de Roches of Winchester was also active in promoting the Carmelite friars, who arrived with him in England in 1241. Founded as far back as c1154 by St Berthold, this order was orginally a grouping together of various small communities of hermits in the Holy Land. Officially known as the Order of Our Lady of Mount Carmel (after a place of that name in Palestine) they became known as the White Friars from the cloaks that they eventually adopted. Originally this order was dedicated to contemplation. After it became more orientated to preaching and teaching in the 1250s some members broke away and for a while maintained a few of their own separate and secluded houses, being known as Pied Friars from their multi-coloured cloaks. Including a few Pied Friars' houses there were about forty houses of Carmelites in England.

The Order of Friars of St Augustine (sometimes known as the Austin Friars or the Friars Eremites) was created to bring together under one rule various communities of hermits. It obtained equality with the three other main orders of friars in 1241 and by 1248 had a house at Clare in Suffolk, the only one of their 34 English houses where significant remains can be seen by the public. From 1289 Augustinian friars could grant indulgences of 100 days for those visiting their churches on certain feast days, and from 1302 they were allowed to bury lay men and women in their cemeteries.

Two other orders of friars which survived in England through to the Reformation of the 1530s, although with only a few houses each, were the Friars of the Holy Cross, usually known as the Crutched Friars, and the Trinitarians or Friars of the Holy Trinity for the Redemption of Captives, originally established in France for bringing back from the Holy Land fighting men taken prisoner by the Saracens, and later associated with local poor relief. Both orders were involved in the running of hospitals and tended to have only small communities, Trinitarian houses usually having a minister or prior, three clerks and three lay brothers, as laid down by their rules. They seem to have arrived in England early in the 13th century and sometimes took over older establishments.

Under a decree of the Council of Lyons in 1274 some other smaller orders, such as the Friars of the Penance of Jesus Christ (founded in 1245 and usually known as the Friars of the Sack from their chosen costume) were forbidden to take on any fresh recruits so that their communities died out in the early 14th century, their possessions passing to colleges, hospitals or other religious institutions. The first of their 14 English houses was founded in 1257. Rye has possible standing remains of one of them.

The Trinitarians sometimes took over older established hospitals. Most of their ten houses were in rural locations, and had endowments to bring in some regular income from estates and the tithes and dues of appropriated churches that they served. This was the norm for houses of monks and regular canons and necessary for Trinitarian friars to fulfil their aims of local charitable works and bringing home crusaders taken prisoner by foreign powers. The other orders of friars were mendicant (beggars) and were not supposed to hold property apart from the land on which their house, cemetery, gardens and water supply were located. Sometimes they even had to pay rents on parts of these and it was generally accepted that friars continually had to beg for alms as well as preach. Thus the mendicant friars usually had to rely on the continued generosity of local benefactors both for building works and everyday subsistance and much of the recorded history of each friary that survives concerns such benefactions, most of them quite small, with prayers for benefactors usually expected in exchange.

Henry III and Edward I frequently donated oaks from royal forests for building works, allowed fuel collecting on royal land, and often gave money for food to supplement supplies of vegetables, fruit and honey produced in friary gardens. Our records of the numbers of friars present in each establishment from time to time is largely based on these grants for food, a fixed sum of 4d usually being allowed for each friar. Other royal grants were made when a friary was hosting a provincial chapter of its order and its resources to accommodate and feed everyone attending were stretched to the limit.

A few friars from each community would be licensed by the bishop of the see to preach and hear confessions whenever and wherever they felt like it. Sometimes there was jealousy from older monastic houses in the area because of the competition for gifts and patronage. Local clergy sometimes complained that friars gave absolution after confession too easily and insisted on all payments due on burials, even if the deceased was actually buried in a friary church or cemetery. Generally speaking, however, the bishops actively supported the friars' activities in their dioceses.

Friars were noted for teaching and played a considerable part in the development of the universities at Oxford and Cambridge during the mid 13th century. By 1300 this too was causing friction since friars expected be able to study for theology degrees without doing seven years of study on an arts degree first, which the University authorities demanded, but which was supposed to be prohibited for members of houses of friars by nature of their chosen profession. From 1304 onwards the crown made an annual grant to help support the numerous student friars in some convents, particularly those of Oxford and Cambridge. Student friars also tended to rely upon finding lay patrons to purchase the books that they needed. Once trained after a period in a friary some friars ended up serving in lay households as clerks, teachers, medics and confessors. Despite their mendicant status some friars had influence and a few became bishops.

A few Franciscans studied old Greek and Hebrew texts of books of the Bible and their translations and interpretations eventually caused them to challenge some of the accepted views of the church. One or two were denounced as heretics and tried in papal courts. There was a particular rivalry between the Franciscans and the Dominicans who were noted as being more orthodox and less obsessed with absolute poverty. At Cambridge the Dominicans also clashed with the Carmelites over the latter's claim (which was upheld) to add "of the Mother of God" to their title. The influx of students sent from mother convents swelled the numbers of friars in some of the Oxford and Cambridge houses up to about the 60 mark but other houses usually had thirty to forty friars. By 1300 there may have been as many as 5,000 friars living in England.

*Preaching cross near the
Dominican friary at Hereford*

The Blackfriars Arts Centre at Boston

Insofar as their studies, teaching and outside preaching activities allowed, friars generally had similar daily patterns as those of monks and regular canons, following clearly defined sets of rules. This meant attending several church services, saying prayers for their benefactors' souls and a daily meeting in the chapter house. The main midday meal was taken in silence whist religious tracts were read out by one of their number, other meals being shorter. Well educated friars licensed by the local bishop to preach and hear confessions would spend much time outside the convent, some of it travelling. Novices and lay brothers may have done the cooking, washing and cleaning as friars busy with preaching or study would have little time for menial tasks, although they might practise horticulture. Friars were not supposed to keep servants, especially personal ones, and lacked funds to pay them, except in the Trinitarian houses. Building works were done by lay professionals and usually paid for by rich benefactors who pledged specific sums for certain tasks, or left legacies in their wills, expecting in return rights of burial and prayers and masses to be said for family members.

There was royal concern about the amount of land being permanently handed over to the Church. Soon permission had to be obtained from the Crown and a local enquiry often held before benefactors could donate land for the expansion of friary precincts. In cases where this would have an adverse effect upon local trade or the maintenance or manning of town defences, or where drainage was an issue, permission might be refused. In a few cases a proposed establishment of a new friary never took place or the house finally ended up in a completely different part of the town. The transfer of a friary to a larger or better drained site was common, especially during the 13th century.

Despite provisions made for each friary to be inspected periodically by the head of its grouping there was a tendency for things to become lax later on, especially when communities shrank in size. In the 15th century there was a movement amongst some Franciscans back towards the original strict rules. These friars were known as Observants. King Henry VII was supporter of the Observants and founded or refounded a few new houses for them in the 1490s. The vast majority of English friaries had been founded during the last three quarters of the 13th century, and although a few new houses were founded in England in the 14th century, there were hardly any foundations between 1400 and the 1530s apart from these few Observant Franciscan houses.

Once King Henry VIII (himself an honorary lay-brother of the Trinitarians since 1508) had determined to make the break with the Roman church over the matter of his divorce from Catherine of Aragon the fate of the monasteries was sealed. Friaries were specifically excepted from the acts of Parliament under which the smaller monastic houses were suppressed in 1535-37. Most of the friaries were surrendered to Henry VIII's commissioners during the second half of 1538 although one or two communities lasted until 1539. By then most of the communities outside of Oxford and Cambridge were reduced down to a dozen or less, not including lay brothers and servants. A few friars did oppose the king's take over of the church but most of these fled abroad just before their houses were visited by the commissioners and then surrendered.

Compliant monks were normally pensioned off from funds available from rich monastic estates, but poverty-stricken mendicant friars were usually turned out without any pension. Some eventually found roles in the running of hospitals and schools and others with preaching skills were sometimes appointed to benefices of local churches as they became vacant. Most of the friary buildings were found by the king's commissioners to be rather bare inside. Inventories for some list items such as vestments, chalices, a table or two, a handful of beds, and basic kitchen equipment. On the whole friaries, particularly those of the Carmelites and Franciscans, had adhered to their aims of obsolute poverty, and some communities were rather in debt when dissolved. Letters and lists drawn up by the king's commissioners also show that many of the friary buildings were in a poor state of repair by the 1530s and even the value of their materials was limited, most of them having little or nor lead on the roofs. Often donations from townsfolk had dried up, forcing friars to lease out portions of their precincts.

With the relaxation of laws against Catholicism in the 19th century friars have returned to England. Amongst others Camelites are back in residence at Aylesford, and Augustinians at Clare, and there are Dominicans again in Cambridge, although not on the medieval site, which is now a college, and also in London, again on a new site.

Cloister arcade remaining from the Dominican friary at Hereford

FRIARY BUILDINGS

Almost all friaries in England were located within towns or just outside their walls or bounds. Many towns had two or three friaries, Boston, Chester, Norwich and Sleaford each had four, and Berwick, Bristol, Cambridge, Lincoln, London, Oxford, Newcastle-upon-Tyne, Northampton and Oxford all had as many as five or six. Usually friars originally settled on quite small plots of land which were later enlarged by adjacent plots being purchased or given by benefactors. Initially friars sometimes built small oratories and made do with modest timber-framed buildings or older pre-existing structures but by the 1260s most communities had substantial buildings of stone under construction and quite a few had begun stone churches back in the 1230s or 40s. Piecemeal enlargement folloowing the acquisition of more land was common and total rebuilding later on, sometimes after a fire, flood or a change of site, was quite common.

At the Reformation both the lands and the materials of former friary buildings close to town centres were too valuable to be left alone. Most English friaries were dismantled quite soon after being suppressed and the sites re-redeveloped. The few standing remains are mostly instances of where parts of the building survived through being made into Elizabethan mansions or were adapted as some sort of civic buildings or industrial premises. Two thirds of all English friaries have vanished without trace and in several cases even their exact locations are uncertain. Only at about a quarter of the sites of the English friaries is significant information available about the size, shape, layout and dating of the buildings, either from excavations or from standing remains usually in a much altered and restored condition. The picturesque ruined friaries still standing almost complete in the western parts of Ireland, where friars often managed to linger for a century or more after the Reformation (and the locals remained mostly catholic), have few parallels in England. Hulne in Northumberland and Walsingham in Norfolk with their fairly rural surroundings are the nearest English equivilents. Both have lost some important rooms and neither now retains a church tower.

The aisled nave of the Dominican friary church at Norwich

Norwich has the only English friary church to have survived intact, apart from the loss of its tower and some alterations to adapt the aisled nave as a public hall. A parish church shared by Trinitarian friars remains complete at Ingham. Complete roofed friary choirs have survived at Chichester and Atherstone, the latter having an unusual central tower with octagonal upper parts. At Reading a much rebuilt aisled nave remains in use. A fair amount survives of two friary churches at Gloucester, one very heavily altered into a house and minus both ends but preserving parts of the original roof, the other a defaced nave and aisle now lacking a choir. There are central towers but little else still standing of friaries at Coventry, King's Lynn and Richmond in Yorkshire. Excavations have laid bare the footings of the choir at a second friary in Coventry. Footings of another choir have been left exposed at Bridgnorth, where a crypt was provided underneath because of the steep fall of the site. The only other known crypt in an English friary church was at Great Yarmouth. An polygonal apsed east end remains at Winchelsea. Fragmentary ruined remains of churches remain at Arundel, Burnham Norton, Clare, Ipswich, Kings Langley and Thetford and parts remain embedded in later buildings at Cambridge, Rye and Thetford.

Franciscan friary church at Gloucester

Excavations have located sufficient remains of the layouts of churches at Aylesford, Bridgwater, Lichfield, London, Oxford and Warrington but none now remain exposed.

The choir of a friary church was usually without aisles or flanking chapels or vestries and was reserved for the friars' private services. The naves were effectively preaching boxes for laity and were usually visually separate internally, although under one overall roof. Some of the naves were rebuilt with aisles in the 14th century, those at Norwich and Coventry attaining great size. Naves at Bridgwater, Ipswich, Lichfield, London, Reading, Walsingham, and Winchelsea are also known to have had north and south aisles with arcades of five or six bays or more. The Franciscan church in London was enormous, being fifteen bays long with both the nave and choir fully aisled.

By the 14th century the custom had arisen of creating a passage or walking place between the nave and choir of a friary and above this sometimes rose a tall slender tower. Friaries did not usually have western towers like parish churches nor true cruciform plans with central towers as wide as the four arms of the building. No English friary church retains an early tower, nor are there any of the long rows of conjoined single lancets of the type seen in the 13th century choirs of Irish friaries in urban locations. However a church of c1269-82 at Chichester has an east window of five stepped lancets and side windows with early Decorated style tracery. In England friary church remains surviving above foundation level tend to be later, ie early 14th century at Reading, the 1370s at Atherstone, and c1440-70 (and the 1340s) at Norwich. The double naved church (unusual in England) at Gloucester is as late as the early 16th century.

Most abbeys had cloisters placed on the south side of the church but in friaries the cloisters were sometimes placed on the north side, as at Atherstone, Bridgnorth, Ingham, Norwich and Richmond and the Franciscan nunnery at Denny. Commonly there was a narrow open space between the church and the cloister of a friary as in the Carmelite house at Coventry and the Franciscan houses at Lichfield and Walsingham. Around the cloister rooms were arranged in two or three ranges usually according to the standard monastic layout, although friaries tended to deviate from it slightly more often. The east range usually had a projecting chapter house and dayroom below a dormitory whilst the range opposite the church often contained the refectory with the kitchen by the corner to the west of it. The west range might contain the prior's room and guest rooms unless a separate block was provided for that purpose. Commonly in friaries one or more of the ranges was narrow on the lower storey, but the upper storey extended over the adjacent cloister walk to give enough width for a dormitory or refectory on the upper level, as at Coventry, Dunwich, Norwich, Walsingham and Ware. A reredorter or latrine block usually projected at one end of the dormitory. The refectory normally had a pulpit built into a recess set in a projection in the outer wall from which one of the brethren would read from the Bible and other approved works during meals so as to discourage the friars from idle conversation across the tables.

In London the houses of the Dominicans and Franciscans each had a second smaller second cloister with the infirmary adjoining one or two sides of it. Much of a secondary cloister still remains at Walsingham, and there appear to been others at Beverley and Lichfield. In other houses the infirmary, bakehouses, guest rooms and other chambers were set around an outer court rather than a proper cloister, although it might have a arcaded walkway of the sort found in a cloister down at least one side, as at Bristol. Remains of one or more of the ranges of buildings around friary cloisters survive roofed but always rather in a rather altered condition at Alyesford, Beverley, Blakeney, Boston, Bristol, Canterbury, Clare, Coventry, Newcastle-upon-Tyne, Norwich, Shrewsbury, Tickhill and Ware and there are ruined ranges at Dunwich, Hereford and Hulne. Part of a cloister walk remains in a house at Hitchin. Other parts away from the main cloister remain of Franciscan friaries at Canterbury, Lichfield and Lincoln. In the fine 14th century east range and adjoining cloister walk at the Carmelite friary at Coventry both the lower rooms and cloister alley are rib-vaulted and there is an truncated chapter house entrance facade. Clare also has the outer walls of a former cloister with a chapter house entrance.

The excavated remains of the friary at Bridgnorth

Old print of Lincoln Franciscan Friary

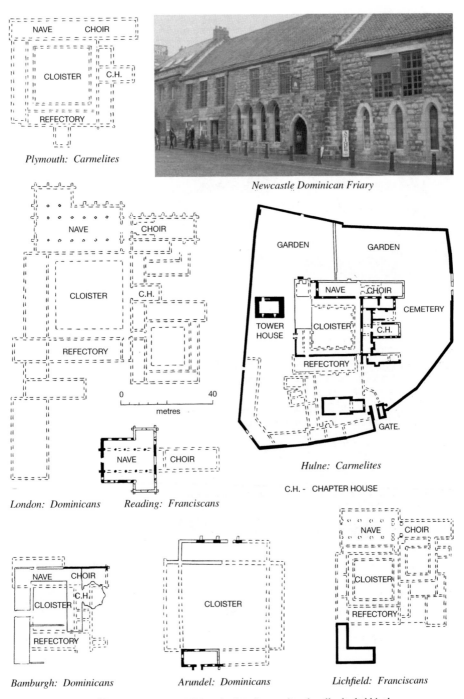

Plymouth: Carmelites

Newcastle Dominican Friary

London: Dominicans   Reading: Franciscans

Hulne: Carmelites

C.H. - CHAPTER HOUSE

Bamburgh: Dominicans   Arundel: Dominicans   Lichfield: Franciscans

Plans of friaries at 1:1600 scale. Standing medieval walls shaded black.

Interior of the south range of the Dominican friary at Bristol

The ruined 13th century chapter house with its row of original lancets at Hulne is the most complete example of such a room in an English friary. The layout of all the extensive outbuildings is known at Hulne, which has a complete set of precinct walls with a gatehouse and also a detached tower house for defence. Other gatehouses remain at Aylesford, Bodmin, and Burnham Norton. More modest gateways survive at Beverley, King's Lynn and Stamford, plus Dunwich, which has a nearly intact precinct wall. The preaching cross of the Dominicans surviving at Hereford is a reminder that much of the friars' preaching was done out in the open.

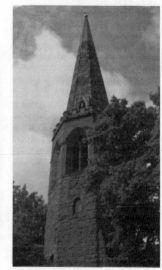

Precinct gateway and west wall of church at Burnham Norton   *Franciscan friary tower at Coventry*

The reredorter or latrine block of the Augustinian friary at Clare

Augustinan Friars' church at Rye

FURTHER READING

Principal sources of historical information about medieval monastic communities are the introductory volumes of the Victoria County Histories, although the series is far from complete. Standing buildings are described in other volumes of that series, and also in over forty volumes of the Buildings of England series by Nikolaus Pevsner and in the county inventories of the Royal Commission on Ancient and Historical Monuments for England, although that series is also far from complete. Most counties have archaeological societies which publish annual journals in which histories and excavations of monastic sites are occasionally described. Brief reports of excavations and other discoveries also appear in Medieval Archaeology. Information has also come from guide books and excavation or renovation reports available for friaries at Aylesford, Bridgnorth, Canterbury, Lichfield, Little Welnetham, Newark, Ware, the nunnery at Denny and also a more general guide to several religious sites at Walsingham.

The SW corner of the main buildings at Aylesford

GAZETTEER OF ENGLISH FRIARIES

APPLEBY Cumbria *Carmelite*   Location Uncertain

Little is known about this friary which was established in 1281 with Lord Clifford and Lord Vesey amongst the patrons, and its location remains uncertain.

ARUNDEL Sussex *Dominican*   TQ 019071   By river bank to east of town

A ruin which was long thought to have been part of the Maison Dieu Hospital is now accepted as having been the south range of a Dominican friary which existed by 1253 and still had five friars when suppressed in 1538. Traces of a former cloister can be seen on the north wall. The dormitory seems to have been in the upper storey of the west range and there appears to have been a large window at its northern end. Part of the buildings formed a malthouse in 1780 and much more of them remained until destruction in the late 19th century. In the grounds on the other side of the road are featureless fragments of the north wall of a range on the north side of the cloister. Most of this part seems to have survived almost complete until at least the 1780s.

ATHERSTONE Warwickshire *Augustinian*   SP 308979   NW of the town centre

The choir and the square crossing supporting a rebuilt octagonal tower date from just after an older chapel here was taken over by Augustinian friars c1375 with Ralph Basset of Drayton as patron. The choir side windows are of three lights and there is a five-light east window with a transom. The church, dedicated to St Mary, remained in parochial use after the friary was closed, although the chancel was later used as a grammar school founded by Sir William Devereux school during Elizabeth I's reign. In the spacious aisled nave of 1849 is a 14th century font with shields showing the emblems of the Passion and the Symbols of the Evangelists. Facing the hall on the site of the friary buildings is a Norman doorway from the former church at Baddesley Ensor.

Remains of the north range, possibly a church, at Arundel

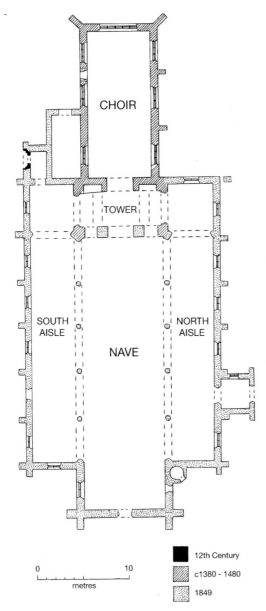

CHOIR

TOWER

SOUTH
AISLE

NORTH
AISLE

NAVE

0   10
metres

	12th Century
	c1380 - 1480
	1849

Plan of the former friary church at Atherstone

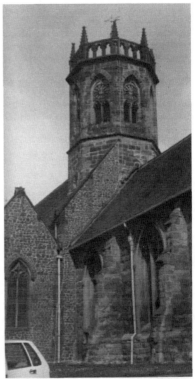

The former friary church at Atherstone

The former friary church at Atherstone

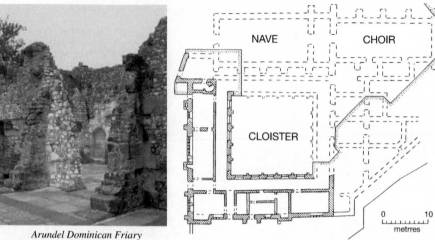

Arundel Dominican Friary

Plan of the Carmelite friary at Aylesford at 1:800 scale

AYLESBURY   Buckinghamshire   *Franciscan*   SU 818138   W side of town centre

This friary was founded in 1387 by James Butler, Earl of Ormond. King Richard II was a benefactor and his successor Henry IV executed one of the friars for his open support of the deposed former king, who had been killed in Pontefract castle in 1400. Nothing remains of the friary, which became a private house after the last seven friars surrendered it to the king in 1538. A house called The Friarage now stands on the site.

The cloister arcades at the Carmelite friary at Aylesford

AYLESFORD   Kent   *Carmelite*   TQ 724589   At west end of village

Founded in 1242 with Ralph Frisburn as chief benefactor, this friary hosted a European General Chapter of the Carmelites in 1247. Of it there survive a gatehouse facing north and the south and west ranges of the claustral buildings which incorporate two of the cloister alleys and which were rebuilt after a fire in 1930. Further alterations and additions were made after the Carmelites re-established a convent here in 1949, which now serves as a conference and retreat centre. In 1951 a relic of St Simeon Stock, d1265 (elected Prior General of the Carmelite Order in 1254) was returned here from where it had been preserved in a convent at Bordeaux.

The gatehouse has a doorway with the date 1590 and initials of John Sedley in the spandrels and the upper windows are of that period, although the main structure is 14th century. The Sedley family took up residence here in the 1570s and they added the outer court or Curia to the SW of the main buildings, although there is a blocked 15th century gateway towards an 18th century brick building at the main cloister NW corner. At the SE corner this outer court incorporates a formerly free-standing guest house which lies on the bank of the River Medway and retains two 15th century doorways. Set above the south walk of the cloister was the refectory in which are traces of a pulpit set in a recess in a projection from the outer wall. There is also the former prior's hall. In the angle between the two ranges was a kitchen with a wide fireplace.

In 1633 the Sedley family sold The Friars to Sir Peter Rycaut, but the property was confiscated by the Parliamentary authorities ten years later after a maid betrayed to Colonel Sandys the Royalist munitions hidden in the roof of the building. Sir Peter was fined £1500 and only recovered possession of the house in 1647. He went bankrupt two years after the unsuccessful Royalist rising in Kent in 1648 and the property was then sold to Sir John Banks. He installed fine ceilings and a staircase lost in the fire.

Excavations have revealed the plan of the medieval church, which was a heavily buttressed and aisle-less building 46m long after being extended in a rebuilding begun in 1348. Cross-walls delineated a walking place between the choir and nave. This area is now used for open air services and has a roofed sanctuary of 1958 with loggias linking it to freestanding chapels on either side.

BABWELL   Suffolk   *Franciscan*

TL 853652   North of Bury St Edmunds

The Franciscans originally established themselves in the NW corner of the town of Bury St Edmunds c1256, when the abbacy of the Benedictine abbey was vacant. In 1263 the monks forced the friars to transfer to a new site at Babwell, beyond the north gate of the town. A new house on the site (now a hotel reached from Mildenhall Road) was built sometime after it was granted to Anthony Harvey in 1542 and the only pre-16th century remains appear to be some parts of the precinct wall. The church was a plain oblong without aisles, its position within the precinct having been located.

The gatehouse at Aylesford

BAMBURGH   Northumberland   *Dominican*   NU 174348   To SW of village

Excavations in 1960 revealed three burials. Traces of the walls of the east and south ranges and reredorter of this friary, which existed by 1295 were located in the 1990s. Paving on the site of the south range includes some re-used architectural fragments. The ruined buildings were mostly demolished in the 19th century and farm buildings of that period now cover most of the site, leaving just one fragment of the buttressed NE corner of the church as the only standing relic. A mid to late 16th century wall built to replace the arcade of the north aisle after it was demolished also survives. With its single narrow aisle, a modest cloister 17m square adjoining the south side of the church, and a chapter room contained within the east range rather than projecting from it, this friary was closer in size and layout to those of Ireland than many of those in England.

BARHAM   Cambridgeshire   *Crutched Friars*   TL 574460   18km SE of Cambridge

Barham Hall of c1830 stands on the site of a house of Crutched Friars established c1293 probably as a small daughter house of the friary at Welnetham in Suffolk with Robert de Furneaux as patron. The small chapel of St Margaret standing on the south side of a cloister survived until the 18th century. It seems to have existed long before the friars arrived and was re-thatched in 1531. The friary was suppressed in 1538.

BARNARD CASTLE   Durham   *Augustinian*   Location Uncertain

In 1381 Archbishop Neville allowed the Augustinians to build a friary and chapel on land which had been donated by Thomas Beauchamp, Earl of Warwick. Old buildings which lay on the east side of Thorngate may possibly have marked the site.

BEDFORD   Bedfordshire   *Franciscan*   TL 044502   To NW of town centre

In c1540 John Leland claimed that Lady Mabel de Pattishall was the founder of this friary, the church of which was dedicated in November 1295, but John St John is more likely to have been the original the founder back in 1238. Land for enlarging the convent was donated in 1310 by some of the townsfolk of Bedford together with the nuns of Harrold. In 1531 the Warden of the recently suppressed friary at Greenwich was sent here for safe keeping. The friary lay by Bromham Road and was surrendered by the warden and vice-warden and ten other friars in 1538. The west range including an alley of the cloister and a building on the north side of the church remained until c1910.

The surviving domestic range at Beverley, now a youth hostel

The SW corner of Blakeney Friary

BERWICK-UPON-TWEED   Northumberland   *Various Orders*   Locations as below

The former Scottish town of Berwick once had five friaries, all founded before it was annexed to England in 1333. King William the Lion established the Trinitarians here in 1214 and Alexander II introduced the Franciscans in 1231, their house being near Low Greens. The Dominicans had a house in the Northumberland Avenue area and the Friars of the Sack were located on the north side of Love Lane. In 2001 traces were found near Palace Street of a Carmelite house founded in 1270 or 1296 by John de Grey.

BEVERLEY   East Yorkshire   *Dominican*   TA 039394   To south of Beverley station

A restoration of the surviving range of this friary founded before 1240 was begun in 1974, and since 1984 it has been in use as a youth hostel. It contains medieval and 16th century wall paintings and has timber-framed internal walls. The brick eastern part must date from a rebuilding with Henry VI as a principal benefactor after the dormitory and library were destroyed by fire in 1449. Also of brick, but probably 16th century, are two gateways, one in Friars Lane and the other moved in the 1960s to the west side of Eastgate. When the friary was suppressed in 1539 the precinct was said be four and half acres in extent. The Warton family had possession from the late 16th century onwards and probably added the projecting wing. The range has a 14th century doorway and was converted into three houses after being sold to the Whiting family in 1827. Excavations from 1960 to 1983 revealed parts of the church and main cloister and a second smaller cloister was discovered during further excavations in 1986-7.

BEVERLEY   East Yorkshire   *Franciscan*   TA 028394   On west side of town

The original Franciscan friary here lay beside Westwood Road, near the former New-biggin Bar. It existed by 1267 when one friar heard the confession of a woman possessed by a devil. In 1291 Archbishop Romanus asked the friars to preach in favour of a new crusade in Driffield, Malton and South Cave. There were 38 friars in 1300 and there were usually over thirty, although their numbers declined in the 1330s. The purchase of lands near the chapel of St Elena in 1297 on behalf of the friars may relate to the eventual transfer of the friary to a new site outside Keldgate Bar, near Queensgate, where it eventually occupied seven acres. Building work there was in progress in 1356 with Sir John Hotham as the main benefactor, he and his descendants being buried in the new church and regarded as the founders until Edward IV's reign when the Warden tried to obtain patronage by granting the title and privileges of founder first to the Nevilles and then to the Percies. In 1407 John Kelk gave 95 merks for repairs to the church and dormitory. The Kelk Chantry set up in the parish church during that period was originally intended for the friary church. One friar, Bonaventura, an Observant brought in from another house, was much in favour of the Pilgrimage of Grace of 1536. Warden Thomas Thomson in February 1539 handed over the friary to the Bishop of Dover.

BLAKENEY   Norfolk   *Carmelite*   TG 032441   To north of Blakeney parish church

In 1296 John and Michael Storm and John and Thomas Thomburn donated a large plot of land to the Carmelites with the consent of Edward I and Sir Wiiliam Roos. The friars were to pray for Sir William and his wife Maud, who had donated 100 merks towards the construction of a church and a hall and kitchen and expected to be able to use a chamber here when in Blakeney. The friars acquired extra land for further buildings in 1316 and 1331. A farmhouse has been formed out of the NW corner of the friary, and parts of the west and south ranges with some old features remain in the outbuildings.

BODMIN Cornwall *Franciscan* SW 062671 In west part of town centre

The only remains of the friary probably founded c1240 are part of a gateway incorporated into a shop in Fore Steet and two piers, one in the graveyard of the parish church and the other in public rooms near Assize Courts on the site of the friary refectory.

BOSTON Lincolnshire *Augustinian* Location Uncertain

This lost friary seems to have stood at the south end of the town on an acre and a half of land donated by John de Hulton, Rector of Skirbeck and John Moser of Leek. The lands were granted to the mayor and burgesses of Boston at the Suppression.

BOSTON Lincolnshire *Carmelite*

TF 327389 To west of River Witham

Lying on a site bounded by the High Street, West Street and Doughty's Quay which was returned to the mayor and burgesses of Boston at the Suppression in the 1530s , this former friary was founded in 1293 or 1301 with Thomas Roos, Earl of Rutland as a major benefactor.

Remains of Bridgnorth Friary as depicted in 1810

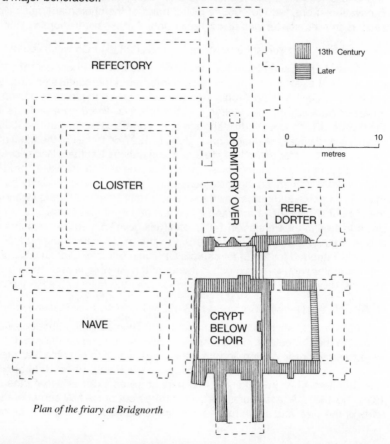

13th Century

Later

REFECTORY

CLOISTER

DORMITORY OVER

RERE-DORTER

0   10

metres

NAVE

CRYPT BELOW CHOIR

Plan of the friary at Bridgnorth

BOSTON Lincolnshire *Dominican* TF 328439 In southern part of town centre

The Blackfriars Hall Arts Centre in Spain Lane to the south of the Market Place (see page 6) is the much restored refectory block 27m long of the friary. Converted into a theatre in 1965, it has several medieval doorways, restored upper windows of two lights, and contains an early 17th century oak staircase brought here from the former Wimbleby Hall at Weston. Another old building with part of a low arcade and traces of vaulting is reached by a 14th century doorway from a passage off South Street. The much restored timber-framed Shodfriars Hall lies to the north but may not actually have formed part of the friary, being more a typical merchant's house. The original buildings of the friary were destroyed in 1288 by a fire that consumed much of the town. A new church at least had been built by 1309. There were 29 friars here in the year 1300.

BOSTON Lincolnshire *Franciscan* TF 331438 To SE of the town centre

Members of the Hanseatic League are said to have founded this friary sometime before 1268 and its church served the Steelyard. The friary probably lay near where the grammar school now is, with a cemetery to the east of the Barditch. Further land for enlargements was obtained in 1322 and 1348. Some of the buildings survived until they were dismantled in 1651.

BRIDGNORTH Shropshire *Franciscan* SQ718935 By the river east of the town

This friary is first mentioned in 1244, when Henry II donated 40 shillings towards work on the church. The site was a cramped one between the River Severn and the foot of the cliffs below the east side of the town just north of the bridge. King Edward I granted the friars six oaks towards building works in 1282. Later benefactors included Nicholas Pitchford, for whom the friars agreed to celebrate two masses in the 1330s, and John Talbot, Earl of Shrewsbury, who was later erroneously stated by John Leland to have been the founder of the friary. In 1538 the last four friars surrendered the friary to Henry VIII's commissioner Richard Ingworth, who described it as the poorest monastic house he had seen "not worth 10s a year, and all the houses falling down". Several old clerical garments, a cross, a lamp, several candlesticks, the bells, two organs, five tables in the refectory and the cooking and brewing utensils were its only contents.

By 1544 the east and north ranges had been made into a house which was granted to John Beaumont and was later held by the Grovenor family but fell into decay. The north or refectory range became an alehouse in the late 18th century (see picture) whilst the rest of the site was used to build river barges. By 1861 the former refectory, still with its reader's pulpit and some original windows, was used as a warehouse by a carpet factory but it was demolished a few years later. By 1989 the carpet factory had gone and the site was excavated prior to houses being built over it. The sandstone lower parts were then exposed of the narrow east range with its projecting reredorter towards the river (now all built over) and the still visible lower part of the eastern half of the church. Here there was a crypt below the choir because of the fall in land level towards the river. Architectural fragments, painted tiles and fragments of stained glass were found in blocking material of the 1540s within a passage with steps down between the two buildings. The east side was set on a platform 45m long projecting 15m out into the river recorded in a court case of 1272 as having been built in the 1250s. This had altered the flow of the river so that it continually damaged the king's mills on the opposite bank. After the Suppression the choir east end was shortened, the crypt gaining a fireplace but losing its vault in order to convert it for domestic purposes.

BRIDPORT   Dorset   *Carmelite*   Location Unknown

In the 1260s the Papal Legate asked the Bishop of Salisbury to allow the Carmelites to hold services in an oratory at Bridport. Their community here seems to have only had a brief life, although in 1365 Sir John Chedeock attempted to re-establish it.

BRIDGWATER   Somerset   *Franciscan*   ST 296367   To south of town centre

Excavations in 2003 revealed parts of the church, which had a total length of 63m and had a central walking place between an aisled nave with a total internal width of 15m and a choir. It was consecrated in 1445 after a rebuilding. Earlier excavations in 1934 had found traces of two buildings, one with floor tiles, some of which lie in the Blake Museum, although others were taken over to Cleeve Abbey. The friary had been founded c1232 by William Brewere, who was soon afterwards buried within it, but in 1245 it moved to a new site which is commemorated in the name Friar Street and was also bounded by West Street and the Durleigh brook. The friars were allowed to acquire another six acres of land in 1349. When suppressed in 1538 the friary had a refectory, kitchen, buttery and several chambers, and the dormitory is mentioned in 1268. By 1571 the surviving buildings had been incorporated into a mansion.

BRISTOL   *Augustinian*   ST 593727   SE of city centre, towards Temple Meads

This friary was founded in 1313 on a 30m square plot of land donated by Sir Simon and Sir William Montacute. The latter provided extra land in 1317 and Thomas de Berkeley gave another four acres of land in 1344. An indulgence of 40 days was granted in 1329 by Ralph de Shrewsbury, Bishop of Bath and Well to those who contributed towards the building of the church. There are no remains of the friary, which in 1538 was surrendered to the king's commissioners by the prior and seven other friars.

BRISTOL   *Carmelite*   ST 584731   To west of the city centre, beyond River Frome

Colston Hall stands on the site of a friary founded c1267 by Prince Edward which lay near a quay beside the River Frome and was later occupied by a grammar school. In 1358 more land was acquired by the friary, which was described by Henry VIII's topographer John Leland just after its suppression in 1538 as the "fairest" of the four friaries at Bristol which had survived into that period. In 1534 there were just four friars left after the prior and sexton had fled after disposing of the friary's plate.

Two views of the Dominican friary buildings at Bristol

BRISTOL   *Dominican*   ST 592733   North of the castle, NE of city centre

This friary in the parish of St James was founded c1228 by Maurice de Gaunt, an altar being dedicated in 1230 by William de Blois, Bishop of Worcester. King Henry III was a generous benefactor and in 1232 allowed the friary to enlarge its burial ground. In 1302 a provincial chapter was held here. Thomas, Lord Berkeley bequeathed £10 in 1532 for the repair of the cloister. Several of the brothers fled abroad in 1534, leaving just the prior and four friars to surrender the friary in 1538.

Two and a half much altered and restored ranges still remain of the cloistral buildings, parts of them having been later used for meetings of the Cutlers Guild and the Quakers. The range on the north originally lay on the south side of the main cloister, north of which lay the church. This range contained the dormitory over day rooms and still has original upper lancets facing north over the former south walk of the cloister plus a two-light west window of c1300 and most of its original roof. A still more impressive old roof with very large wind-braces remains in the half range to the south, where there is a large blocked arch and a projecting chimney breast. The windows on the west side of the east range (which has been widened by 18th century extensions to the east) look as if they once formed part of a second cloister without a north walk.

BRISTOL   *Franciscan*   ST 586733   To NW of city centre, just beyond the walls

After the last six friars had surrendered this friary in 1538 the site in Lewensmead east of St James Priory was claimed for the town by the mayor on the grounds that a group of townsfolk had donated the land on which it was founded in 1234. King Henry III's benefactions to the community included six oaks for building work in 1236.

BRISTOL   *Friars of the Sack*

This community existed by 1266 when King Henry III allowed them six oaks from a royal forest. The church was still in use in 1322 but there is uncertainty as to whether any friars then still remained. Its location is unknown.

BURNHAM NORTON   Norfolk *Carmelite*

TF 838428   0.4km NE of Burnham Market

Near the river lies the west end of the friars' church of St Mary with image niches on either side of a central doorway and remains of corner buttresses. Only humps and bumps remain of the rest of the building. Close by to the west is an early 14th century gateway with flint flushwork with cusped and intersecting tracery patterns, image niches and a rib-vault with bosses showing a lion and an angel blowing a trumpet. A two-light upper window was destroyed by vandals in the 1960s. An early 14th century doorway and other old parts also remain in a nearby farmhouse. The friary was founded in 1241 and was licensed in 1353 for an enlargement of its precinct. See plan on page 24.

Gatehouse at Burnham Norton Friary

CAMBRIDGE   *Augustinian*

TL 448582   South side of city centre

In 1290 Sir Geoffrey de Pitchford, Constable of Windsor, donated land on Peas Hill to the Augustinians in memory of his son Arnulf and subject to an annual rent due to the Crown. In 1292 the convent was allowed to enclose a strip of land 60m long by 9m wide which extended to the town ditch, provided there was a gate at either end to give access for the defence of the town. Pembroke Street, Free School Lane and Corn Exchange Street now bound the site, which had been enlarged by further gifts in 1335 and 1337, and further land was acquired in 1376. During this period the church was repaired and probably enlarged to play an important role in University functions. Traces of it have been found by excavation, along with skeletons of four females (two with children) showing that the right of burial for lay people allowed by the pope in 1302 was here fully exercised. The cloister lay to the south and the friars' own cemetery lay beyond on the other side of a road. Part of what was probably either the infirmary or guest house survived until 1746, and the gateway facing Peas Hill survived nearly to that period, but since then nothing has remained standing.

The gatehouse at Burnham Norton

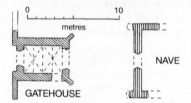

Plan of remains of Burnham Norton Friary

In the early part of Henry V's reign Prior Thomas Cressale and Friar Nicholas Swafham, both Doctors of Divinity, plus two servants, were imprisoned pending payment of fines imposed by the University for their having encouraged their scholars to insult and threaten the Mayor of Cambridge and their imprisonment of one of his officials. On Christmas Eve 1525 Dr Robert Barnes, Prior of the Augustinian friars at Cambridge preached a provocative sermon in favour of reformation of the church in St Edward's church in Cambridge which led to him being brought before Cardinal Wolsey on a charge of heresy. He escaped from imprisonment at Northampton and fled abroad. He was condemned and burned at the stake as a relapsed heretic in 1540 after playing a part in arranging Henry VIII's short-lived fourth marriage to Anne of Cleves.

Another of Dr Barnes group of pro-Reformation Augustinian friars known as 'Little Germany" was Miles Coverdale, who later played an important part in having the Bible translated into English. With so much support for the Reformation within its ranks the community effectively suppressed itself, leaving the prior Dr John Hardyman in charge of the site until it was handed over to the royal commissioners in 1539. Slates from it went for reuse on the new steeple at Great St Mary's in 1545, when most of the friary buildings were demolished. A book of tracts mostly written by Adam de Stockton in 1375 from the friary library mentioned by Leland survives at Trinity College in Dublin.

CAMBRIDGE   Cambridgeshire   *Carmelite*   TL 446583   SW of city centre

In 1249 a group of Carmelite hermits settled at Chesterton. There in 1251 the order's Prior General Simeon Stock is said to have had a vision of Our Lady of Mount Carmel. About five years later most of the community moved to a plot of land they had been given by Michael Malherbe in Newnham. There they reorganised themselves as regular friars with white habits and a normal layout of buildings around a cloister and a communal dormitory. However some of the original hermits who were used to individual cells refused to adopt the changes and became a separate community known as the Brethen of the Blessed Mary. Their attempt to build new premises in 1290 in the parish of All Saints close to the castle brought them into conflict with the canons of Barnwell, with whom an agreement was later reached. These Carmelites continued to use the older 'pied" style of habit. By 1319 they were reduced to just two, Prior William de Fakenham, and Thomas de London, and must have died out shortly afterwards.

In 1290 the main Carmelite community at Newnham moved into the town onto a site between Milne Street and the river. The pretext for this was that during the winter Newnham was cut off from the town by flooding so the friars could not buy food, nor could scholars attend lectures on divinity in their cloister. In 1292 they were allowed to wall their new precinct, subject to it having gates allowing access to the town defences in times of need. In 1315 the enclosing of a lane beside their precinct was allowed, and further extensions were made in 1331, 1347 and 1350, whilst they were also allowed to enclose a spring called Hokerwell outside the town and build an underground aqueduct from it to their convent. They also had custody of the Chest of the Holy Trinity, a fund for subsidising University students set up by the William Bateman, Bishop of Norwich. In 1381 the townsfolk broke into the church and seized this chest, the contents of which were then reckoned to be worth £20. Back in 1375 John Hornby produced documents which convinced a court of the right of the Carmelite friars to add "of the Mother of God" to their title, which had been challenged by the Dominicans.

In 1388, when Parliament met in the Dominican friary at Cambridge, John de Waltham was appointed as Bishop of Salisbury and professed canonical obedience to the Archbishop of Canterbury "in the chapel next the door near the high altar of the Carmelites' church". There was a papal order of 1396 that one Carmelite friar was to be chosen from each of the four Distinctions of London, York, Norwich and Oxford to take a degree of Bachelor or Master in Theology. Following complaints that Carmelites obtained doctorates of divinity too easily Cardinal Landulph ruled that candidates were to study arts for seven years and theology for seven years, and then lecture in a univeristy for several years, starting with the sentences and ending with bible studies.

In 1537 Queen's College obtained from the doomed convent a wall bounding Friars Close for 23 shillings and immediately pierced the wall with a row of new windows. The masters and fellows of Kings College and Queens College were allowed to take over the friary site when the last four friars surrendered it in August 1538, having previously requested this from Thomas Cromwell. The buildings were stripped of their contents and materials between September 1538 and the end of 1539, although the walls stood until 1549, when the tower was taken down in January and the pier bases dug up in March. The furnishings disposed of included covers for just two beds, and the only altar vessel was a "chalyce of tynne", but there were several sets of priests' vestments and no less than 18 copes. The only tangible relics now are fragments of stained glass with incomplete inscriptions and heads of friars in the library of Queen's College, which took over most of the friary site, paying £20 for it to the king.

CAMBRIDGE   Cambridgeshire   *Dominican*   TL 452583   SE of city centre

In 1238 Henry III donated three oaks towards the chapel being built by Dominicans on land they had recently acquired in the parish of St Andrew just outside the Barnwell Gate. The friary soon became the head house of a group of friaries including seven in the diocese of Norwich and several others although there is uncertainty as to whether the prior of Cambridge normally acted as a visitor at the other houses or other clerics were regularly appointed to fulfil this function. Further royal gifts to the Cambridge Dominican friary followed at frequent intervals during the reigns of Henry III and Edward I, and from 1304 onwards it benefited from an annual royal grant made specifically for educational purposes. In the newly enlarged churchyard of the Cambridge friary in 1246 Cardinal William de St Sabina preached to a large crowd on the love of the saints for the Holy Name of Jesus. William Ringesham was the Cambridge Dominicans' first Doctor of Divinity, obtaining his degree c1262 through a faculty first established about ten years earlier. With generous patronage from Alice, widow of Robert de Vere, Earl of Oxford the Dominicans completed their large church by 1286, when it was consecrated by William de Fresney, titular Bishop of Edessa.

A breach opening between mendicant friars and the University led to the Chancellor expelling and excommunicating two Dominicans in 1303. By that time there may have been as many as 200 friars in Cambridge, of which over a third were Dominicans, and the University feared the consequences of large numbers of student friars who did not conform to the norm of studying an arts degree before starting upon theology. A settlement was made by Cardinal Thomas de Jon at Bordeaux stating that although only the University Chancellor or his nominee might preach on Advent Sunday, Septuagesima and Ash Wednesday, yet friars of each order were free to preach at the same time within their own convents, and friars studying Divinity could preach in their own convents instead of St Mary's Church, provided notice was given to the Chancellor.

Three Cambridge Dominicans were amongst the many extra confessors appointed to serve in the Cambridge area by the Bishop of Ely, Thomas Lisle (himself a former Dominican theologian) at the onset of the Black Death. In the autumn of 1388 Parliament met for a month in the Dominican friary at Cambridge, 20 merks afterwards being given to the friars to allow for damage and inconvenience. In 1402 two friars were confined in the Tower of London for supporting the cause of the deposed Richard II.

The 15th century wooden figure of the Virgin Mary in the present Catholic church in Cambridge may be the image which attracted large numbers of pilgrims until August 1538 when Thomas Cromwell permitted Prior Gregory Dodds to remove it. Shortly afterwards Dodds and fifteen other friars surrendered the friary. Dodds had succeeded Prior Oliver, who preached against Henry VIII's divorce from Catherine of Aragon and was moved to Bristol in 1537 and later fled abroad. Another refugee was Robert Buckenham, made Prior of Cambridge in 1526 and sent "to restore the strict observance" of the English Dominicans. His position was made untenable by the royal appointment of John Hilsey, Prior of London, as Master General of the English Dominicans.

Remains of the friary buildings survive in Emmanuel College, which was founded in 1584. The hall range between the two oldest courts of the college was formerly the friary church, although most of its exterior is now ashlar-work of 1764. Original features include two buttresses and parts of several windows visible only internally. Further west is a 15th century archway in a range otherwise mostly of the 1580s. The lower parts also remain of the medieval east range which probably contained the dormitory in the original upper storey, now replaced by work of the 1580s.

CAMBRIDGE   Cambridgeshire   *Franciscan*   TL 450588   In city centre

The Franciscans sent William de Esseby and two others to start a community in Cambridge c1230. They were allowed the use of the site of a former synagogue adjoining a Jew's house which had been taken over by the town for use as a prison. Originally their chapel may have been timber-framed and it was small enough for the roof rafters to have been made and set up within two days. The friars and jailors used a common entrance until in 1238 Henry III granted the Jew's house to the friars and authorised the building of a new prison elsewhere. The convent was allowed to enclose an adjacent lane in 1328 and they were given two further messuages to enlarge their precinct in 1353. The Cambridge house was one of three Franciscan communities annually given a royal grant from 1304 onwards in recognition of its importance as an educational establishment. Other occasional royal grants usually reckoned on a basis of a groat per friar suggest that there were mostly between 55 and 61 friars here. The three main Cambridge friaries were closely involved in the establishment c1250 of a faculty of Theology at Cambridge, although it was common practice for friars seeking degrees to spend periods of study at both Oxford and Cambridge. Students had to deposit a pledge or "caution" as a surety that they would complete their course. Often this took the form of a book being provided by a lay sponsor. Franciscans beginning theology degrees always paid a fine as an alternative to feasting the University authorities.

The Franciscans were involved in the study of Greek and Hebrew biblical sources during the late 13th century, which was the time of Roger Bacon. At Cambridge the Franciscans led the University in opposition to Pope John XXII and in 1329 several of them were confined in their own friary and then sent to the papal court for trial.

Not all Cambridge friars were students and some undertook the joint roles of begging and preaching in the surrounding village, as is recorded in the rare survival of accounts of 1363 and 1366 now bound together with a Codex Leicestrensis of the New Testament which once belonged to Richard Brinkley, who was appointed Provincial Minister in 1524. The accounts record gifts of food, but more usually money, in return for prayers for the donors or their families or friends. The foundation of a small Franciscan house at Ware in 1350 partly encroached on the sphere of influence of the Cambridge Franciscans and adversely affected their income, and in 1395 the Pope ordered limits set on how far out the friars of Ware could preach and beg for alms.

In 1539 two dozen Franciscan friars signed the deed of surrender and they and the servants dispersed before the royal valuers arrived to find very little left of note apart from the lead roofs and three bells in the tower. The survival of at least eight books annotated with Cambridge Franciscan students' notes in pencil in the Ottoboni collection in the Vatican Library suggests that some of the friars managed to leave with their books. The University unsuccessfully petitioned both Thomas Cromwell and Henry VIII for possession of the friary church, which had been greatly enlarged in the early 14th century and was regularly used for staging the ceremonies involved in the conferring of B.A. degrees on Ash Wednesday, and M.A. and higher degrees on St Peter's Day. The whole of the University attended and this required the assembly of temporary wooden staging in the form of an arena which appears to have still been in place in the church when the friars left. By 1547 the buildings had all been dismantled and parts of them were re-used in the chapel of Trinity College. The college named after Lady Frances Sidney, Dowager Countess of Sussex, founded by her in 1594, now lies on the site. Excavations have, however revealed parts of the footings of the nave of the church with its north and south aisle and a shallowly projecting chapel on the north side.

CAMBRIDGE   Cambridgeshire   *Friars of the Sack*   TL 448579   To S of city centre

These friars were established in Cambridge by 1258 and had a small chapel in the parish of St Mary in the Market. They later transferred to a site close to where the Fitz-William Museum now stands, having been allowed in 1253 buy a stone house with a court and chapel from John le Rus who was deeply in debt. The friars built a new church in which was a side-altar of St Lucy, to whom the chapel which it replaced had been dedicated. When in 1307 the community petered out through lack of recruits as ordained by the Council of Lyons in 1274 their lands and buildings were transferred to the neighbouring college of Peterhouse.

CANTERBURY   Kent   *Augustinians*   TR 150576   On SE side of city centre

In 1318 Edward II allowed Archbishop Walter Reynolds to give the Austin friars two acres of land in the parish of Westgate, Canterbury on which to build a house. By 1320 there were eight friars here. A few years later they moved to a new site in St George's parish, in the eastern part of the city, although this initially caused friction with the monks of Christchurch until an agreement was made for payments to both the monks and the parish priest. Further land around this new site, which eventually took up an acre and a half, was acquired in 1329, 1335, 1344 and 1352, the latter being used for the construction of an outer gate facing the Cloth Market. In 1408 Henry IV allowed the friars to rebuild some houses facing the street and to let them out. This would provide some regular income to pay the dues agreed back in 1326 and help with work on friary buildings. They had recently closed off two winding lanes adjoining their land which were then only being used by the citizens for depositing rubbish and filth, which was a health hazard and the smell offended those using the friary church.

There are many records of citizens being buried in the friary church and of bequests and legacies. Elizabeth de Burgh was a benefactor in the 1360s. William Haut of Bish-opsbourne was buried between his wives in front of the image of St Catherine in 1462, and in 1504 Didier Bargier, rector of St Andrews left to the altar of St Didier "my little brevet mass-book covered with red leather". In 1522 the friars agreed to provide a chaplain to say a daily mass for the souls of Sir John Fineux, Chief Justice of Common Pleas, and his wife Elizabeth. Sir John had spent more than £40 on repairs to the church, refectory, domitory and precinct walls. On the feasts of the Assumption, St Cyprian and St Crispin the members of the "Gild of the Assumption of our Lady of the Crafts and Misteries of the shoemakers, curriers and cobblers" were bound by a 1518 ordinance to attend masses in the friary church. When there were disputes to be settled between the monks of the abbey of St Augustine and the citizens the latter paid the friars for providing lodging for the arbitrators brought in from outside.

Despite all these benefactors the friars were in debt by as much as £40 when the friary was surrendered to the Bishop of Dover in December 1538, and the contents of the friary were only worth about £6. Friar John Stone "very rudely and traitorously used himself" and "declared he was ready to die for it that the king might not be head of the Church, but it must be a spritual father appointed by God". Still surviving from 1539 are records of payments totalling about thirteen shillings to his executioner, the erectors of the gallows and the wood and cord that was used to make them, to the men that parboiled the poor friar in a "kettle" and a woman that scoured it afterwards, and to the men that hung up the severed quarters of his body upon the city gates.

Excavations in 2000-01 found traces of the clay floors of the kitchen, refectory and warming room, a piece of stained glass, and a rare fragment of medieval parchment.

The guest-house of the Dominican friary at Canterbury

CANTERBURY Kent *Dominicans* TR 149581 On north side of city centre

In 1237 Henry III granted the Dominicans an island in the River Stour for a friary. Further gifts over the next 23 years by the king and queen towards building works totalled nearly £500. By 1243 the church was sufficiently complete to be dedicated to St Edward the Confessor and a kitchen was built in 1259 at a cost of £20. In 1275 an inquisition recorded that the friars had enlarged the island in such a way as to cause damage by the river to the king's mills but no action was taken against them. Royal grants for food from 1297 to 1302 suggest that there were about 30 friars at that time. In 1299 Thomas, rector of Chartham gave them some more land, and they acquired further plots of land in 1319.

A provincial chapter of the order was held at Canterbury in 1394. Tents used to stage feasts on three successive days were lashed by stormy weather. The archbishop sponsored the first feast, the second was at the joint expense of the abbot of St Augustine's and the prior of Christchurch, and the third was staged by the lords of Kent. In 1535 Archbishop Thomas Cranmer preached against the authority of the Pope in the cathedral and the Dominican prior got into trouble for preaching the opposite cause. The friary was surrendered to the Bishop of Dover in December 1538 and for a while it seems to have been used by John Batehurst for cloth making until sold in 1560. Most of the buildings seem to have survived until the 18th century. What was described in 1356 as "our new gate" stood at the end of Friars Way in St Peter's Street until it was taken down in 1787. Built of squared flint, it had a niche with a statue of St Dominic.

A plan of 1595 shows the church lying on the south side of a cloister and extending well to the east of it. Unusually the dormitory was in the north range, whilst the mid 13th century west range, which still survives on the river bank and was restored in 1983, contained a refectory with a pulpit set over a low undercroft with parts of the rib-vault rebuilt in the 16th century in brick. The undercroft piers are square with chamfered corners. The upper windows have paired lancets with quatrefoils between the heads and there is an original 13th century roof with double collars and crown-posts on tie-beams. Within the Methodist meeting house of 1763-4 adjoining the south end is part of the NW corner of the friary church. Aligned east-west on the opposite bank of the river is what is thought to have been the friary guest house, a much altered and rebuilt 14th century structure.

CANTERBURY   Kent   *Franciscans*   TR 147577   Near middle of city centre

Canterbury was one of the places where Franciscans first settled after they arrived in England in 1224, but they only seem to have established their own permanent buildings after 1268 when Alderman John Diggs gave them a plot he had just purchased on an island in the River Stour to the SW of the Dominican friary. The only surviving building is a structure of that period built on arches over a branch of the river and probably used as the warden's lodging. A doorway over Greyfriars Passage further north is a meagre relic of the walking place between the choir and the nave of the church. In 1294 the friars agreed to pay to the monks of Christchurch a yearly rent of three shillings for the use of tenements recently taken into the friars' precinct. During this period there are several records of the monks at Christchurch employing a Franciscan as a lecturer at their convent. In 1309 the Franciscans were allowed to build a bridge over the river to allow public access to their church, which was consecrated by Archbishop Reynolds in 1325. By that time the number of friars here seems to have risen to an average of about thirty five.

In 1338 two of friars received a royal pardon for the rescue of two felons being taken to a place of execution. Amongst those buried in their church was a younger son of John Balliol, former king of Scotland, and Bartholomew de Badlesmere, hanged here in 1322 by Edward II after he refused to admit Queen Isabella to Leeds Castle, then in his charge. Canterbury was one of the few Franciscan houses that adopted the more strict Observant rule in the 1490s under encouragement of Henry VII, who in 1509 generously bequeathed the friars 100 marks, whilst another £200 for their use (presumably for building works) was entrusted to the prior of Christchurch. A provincial chapter was held in Canterbury in 1532. Two years later two of the friars were executed at Tyburn along with the Maid of Kent for supporting the cause of Queen Catherine of Aragon. The king then appointed John Arthur as Warden at the priory, where he was unpopular. He fell from grace over an accusation that he had preached a sermon that lamented that new books and new preachers were discouraging pilgrimages, especially to St Thomas Becket's shrine, and he was forced to flee to France to avoid being starved.

In 1539 the site was sold to Thomas Spilman, and then had a church with a bell-tower, along with two orchards, two gardens, three acres of land, five acres of meadow and four acres of pasture. By the 1570s the Lovelace family had possession and they retained it for many years. In the British Museum in London are several 13th and 14th century books which came from the library of the Franciscans at Canterbury. They include a copy of Geoffrey of Monmouth's Historia Britonum.

CANTERBURY   Kent   *Friars of the Sack*   TR 144577   West of the city centre

In 1289 and 1293 Edward I paid for three days food for three friars here, but they died out a few years later. A tenement here in St Peter's Street was long known as the Houses of the Friars of The Sack.

CARLISLE   Cumbria   *Dominican*   NY 400558   On west side of city centre

The Dominicans were settled here by 1237, when they were permitted to make a hole in the city wall to bring in a water supply. In 1239-44 Henry III granted them timber from Inglewood Forest for work upon their church. The buildings were destroyed by a fire that affected much of the city in 1292. Shortly after the friars left in 1538 the friary was surrounded by a new paling to serve as a council chamber and as a magazine and store for the garrison.

The warden's lodging at Canterbury Franciscan Friary

Refectory range, Canterbury Dominican Friary

CARLISLE Cumbria *Franciscan* NY 401559

In the middle of the city centre

Friars Court behind Devonshire Street lies on the site of the Franciscan house here, which also suffered from the fire of 1292 and had been founded back in the 1230s. Edward I occasionally stayed in the friary and granted it six oaks for building works in 1280. Little else appears to be known about it.

Canterbury Franciscan Friary

CHELMSFORD Essex *Dominican* TQ 708069 To south of the town centre

There appears to be no record of the founding of this friary, which lay on the south side of the River Wid in the parish of Moulsham. Here in the 1320s was trained the noted scholar Thomas of Langford. In 1341 the friars acquired three extra acres of land and were allowed to make a conduit over the well forming their water supply. In 1538, when the friary was surrendered to the Bishop of Dover, there is a mention of the choir and chapels, the cloister, vestry, frater, buttery, kitchen and brew-house.

CHESTER Cheshire *Carmelite* SJ 404661 In the middle of the city centre

In 1279 Thomas Stadham founded this friary, which lay on a site bounded by Weaver Street, Commonhall Street, Whitefriars and Bridge Street. Opposition to the Carmelites arrival here was dispelled when an image of the Virgin in the abbey miraculously pointed them out as chosen brethren. In 1367 the community had a prior, sub-prior, reader and eleven other friars. In 1386-98 more Carmelites were ordained in Chester than the Dominicans and Franciscans put together. There were ten friars here when the friary was surrendered in August 1538. At that time there were five altars in the choir. After the site was acquired in 1592 by the Attorney General, Thomas Egerton, the church was demolished and the rest replaced by (or possibly incorporated in) a new house.

CHESTER   Cheshire   *Dominican*   SJ 402660   On SW side of city centre

The Dominicans may have used a pre-existing chapel of St Nicholas when they first arrived in Chester in 1236. They were allowed in 1276 to pipe in water through the city wall to their friary which was bounded on the south by Watergate Street and on the east by Nicholas Street. Fifteen friars of this house were ordained as licensed preachers during the bishopric of Roger Northburgh from 1321 to 1358 and it enjoyed royal patronage from Richard II in the 1380s. The prior and friars were accused in 1454 of attacking a servant of the Abbot of Chester as part of a typical dispute between monks and friars. In 1464 it was alleged that a Dominican friar had killed a local baker, and another was charged in 1495 with having stabbed the Carmelite prior. The nave of their church seems to have become disused by August 1538, when the friary was dissolved. At that time there is a mention of the frater, dorter, chambers for the prior and sub-prior, a chamber over the church doorway, a new chamber, and the kitchen and the old and new butteries. Excavations in 1976-8 found traces of the church and the water supply system, plus evidence of two outbuildings to the north of the church.

CHESTER   Cheshire   *Franciscan*   SJ 401663   On west side of city centre

This friary to the north of Watergate Street is first mentioned in 1235 as newly established with the support of the Bishop of Lincoln. The gatehouse faced the street named after the new linen hall built over the site in 1778. The church was 60m long and had a steeple and an aisled nave which had fallen out of use by 1528, when local merchants were allowed to store sails and other equipment for ships within it. It had been converted into a dwelling by the early 17th century. Little is recorded about the friars here apart from an assault on their warden in 1427, and the surrender of the friary by seven friars in August 1538.

CHESTER   Cheshire   *Friars of the Sack*   Location Unknown

Little appears to be known about this community, which existed by 1274 but may have died out by c1300.

Choir of the Franciscan friary at Chichester

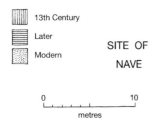

13th Century

Later

Modern

SITE OF

NAVE

0   10

metres

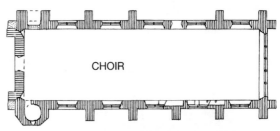

CHOIR

Plan of the Franciscan friary church at Chichester

CHICHESTER   West Sussex   *Dominican*   SZ 865049   To east of the city centre

The Dominicans were established here by 1283 when Prior William got into trouble for celebrating mass in a church at Steyning which Archbishop Peckham had placed under an interdict. Edmund, Earl of Cornwall allowed them to acquire more land in 1284. When the court was in Chichester the following year Queen Eleanor purchased a strip of land next to the Dominican friary and handed it over to the friars. In 1289 they made a new street between St Andrew's church and the city wall, their buildings having by then been built across two older streets. Edward allowed them to acquire more land in 1310. There were thirty-four friars in 1297, but only twenty-one in 1324. The friary was surrendered in October 1538 by Prior John Anteny and a few other friars to Richard Ingworth, Bishop of Dover.

CHICHESTER   West Sussex   *Franciscan*   SZ 863051   In NE part of city centre

The Franciscans arrived here soon after 1225 and in 1253 were given extra land by Henry III's brother Richard, Earl of Cornwall. However in 1269 they moved to the present site, now known as Priory Park but originally part of the outer bailey of the castle. The buildings were recorded as being in good repair when surrendered by the last seven friars in 1538, and the choir of the church still remains roofed and in use for arts displays. Probably dating from c1270-82, and the second oldest friary church still roofed in England, (after a much altered one at Gloucester) it has five windows on each side with two pointed lights under a quatrefoil and the east wall has five tall stepped lancets under an outer arch. The outer lights were shortened and given cusps when a new wagon woof was provided in the 15th century. Inside are a plain piscina, sedilia and a tomb recess. At the SW corner is a turret containing a stair up to a lost tower. A blocked arch faces west towards where there was an aisle-less nave of about the same length. The cloister and its buildings probably lay to the north, where there is one slight fragment of the infirmary.

Lavatorium arches at Clare Friary

House converted from the west range of Clare Friary

CLARE   Suffolk   *Augustinian*   TL 771450   Just south of the castle remains

This was the first and is now the most complete of the Augustinian friaries in England, being founded in 1248 by Richard de Clare, Earl of Gloucester. When surrendered in 1539 the friary occupied as much as 38 acres and its west range was then adapted as a mansion in which the Frende and then the Barker families lived for many generations until Augustinians returned to re-occupy it in 1953. This range has a 14th century doorway and contains a vaulted chamber at the south end but it also has low windows with arched lights and a ceiling of the early 16th century when the upper storey was remodelled as the prior's residence. One mullioned and transomed window and an added bay are late 16th century and there is fine 17th century panelling upstairs.

The church had a narrow central tower between a five bay nave and a six bay choir that inclined to the north. The south walls of each part remain fairly complete with a doorway to the cloister under the tower and a doorway further east to a vestry. The choir has sedilia with cusped blank arches against the back wall. Cutting into them is an arch inserted to take the tomb of Edward I's daughter, Joan of Acre, wife of Earl Gilbert de Clare, who was buried here in 1307. She added the chantry chapel of St Vincent adjoining this side east of the vestry. Excavations have shown that the nave had a north aisle with a five bay arcade and then a chapel of the Annunciation beside the central tower seems to have extended northwards as a transept.

Joan's daughter Elizabeth de Burgh was also a great benefactor of the friary, and had two friars sing mass daily in the chapel of the adjacent castle in return for supplies of wheat and malt. She sponsored the construction of the cloister and its buildings, the dormitory, chapter house and refectory all being dedicated in 1380, whilst the church had been dedicated back in 1328. The refectory lay on the south side, a later fireplace breast having replaced the former reader's pulpit. In the south cloister walk near the refectory doorway is an arched lavatorium (see page 33) where the friars could wash their hands before meals. There is a tiny court in the SW corner with timber-framed cloister walks on the south and west side of it, this part having remained in use as part of the house created from the west range. A kitchen also lay in this area.

The dormitory lay on the upper floor of an east range that very unusually was separated from the main cloister by a narrow court. The chapter house thus projected west from this range instead of east and its fine entrance doorway from the cloister survives. A range that may have served as part of the infirmary connected the dormitory to the reredorter further east, all these parts having diagonal corner buttresses.

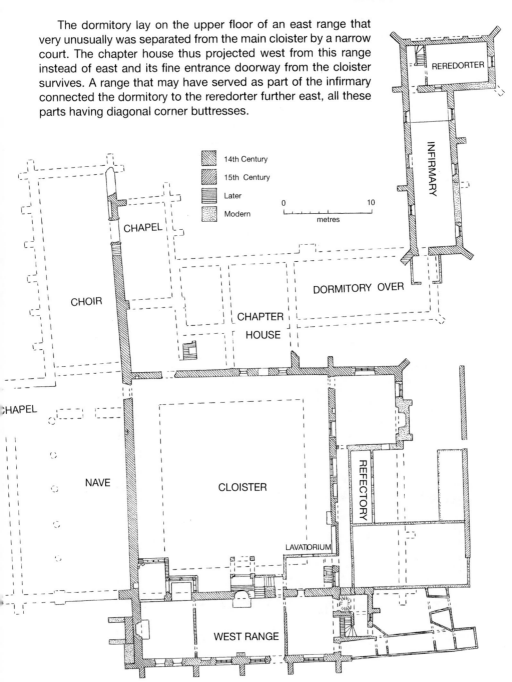

Plan of Clare Friary

COLCHESTER   Essex   *Crutched Friars*   TL 991249   Beyond SW corner of town

This was originally a hospital mentioned as early as 1235, but the master later squeezed out the brethren serving it and introduced friars instead. Their community seems to have died out but four crutched friars reclaimed the premises in 1496. Excavations in 1989 before an office block was built on the site found traces of one large building.

COLCHESTER   Essex   *Franciscan*   TM 001252   In the SE part of walled town

The earliest record of the Franciscans here is in 1279 when Edward I allowed them to build a conduit through his lands and the town wall to supply the friary with water from a well recently donated by Nicholas de la Warde. Robert Fitz-Walter donated land in 1309 and laid the foundations of a new church, finally joining the community as a brother in 1325. More land was acquired in 1338. Sir John Gernon and his wife Margaret were buried on the north side of the choir in 1380. Also buried here in 1407 was Nicholas Faklenham, who in 1395 had become the provincial of the order.

COVENTRY   Warwickshire   *Carmelites*   SP 340787   To SE of the city centre

Sir John Poultney established the Carmelites on this location in 1342, although they may have previously had a community elsewhere in Coventry. Massive footings of the six bay long choir of have been revealed and left uncovered. Originally a rectangular central tower was planned but the tower eventually built (which collapsed in 1572) was a proper square and flanked by shallow transepts with diagonal corner buttresses. In 1384 Lord Basset of Drayton left £300 in his will towards construction of the fully aisled nave nine bays long with slender lozenge-shaped arcade piers, nothing of which remains visible, although excavations prior to new road-building have found parts of it, along with considerable quantities of old tiles and glass. The completion of this part in the early 15th century resulted in a church 90m long externally, probably second in size amongst friary churches only to that of the Greyfriars in London. The nave east end had chapels on either side of a passage through to the crossing under the tower.

East range of the Carmelite friary at Coventry

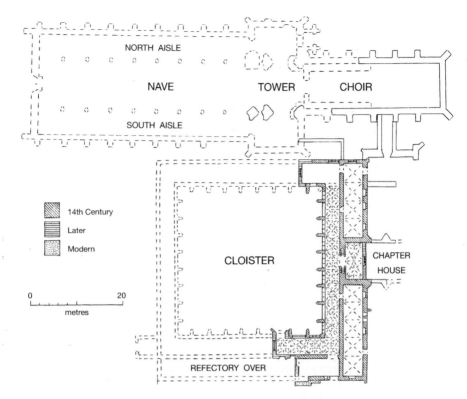

Plan of the Carmelite friary at Coventry at 1:800 scale

The Coventry Carmelites obtained more land in 1413 and in 1506 were left 20 marks in the will of Thomas Bonde towards work on the cloister which lay to the south. During this period the guilds of the carpenters and smiths held annual feasts in the friary hall, presumably the refectory. Prior High Burnby and thirteen friars surrendered the friary to Dr London in October 1538. After being sold by Sir Ralph Sadler to John Hales in 1544 the east range was converted into a mansion with new mullion and transom windows and a west-facing oriel window on the upper storey. Here John Hales (d1572) entertained Queen Elizabeth I who described the accommodation as "commodius" and is said to have addressed the citizens of Coventry from the oriel window.

In 1801 the mansion was sold and the east range became a workhouse until the 1940s, after which it served as a Salvation Army hostel. The lower storey is rib-vaulted and has several original 14th century two light windows, plus the western bay of the projecting chapter house probably three bays long with stairs rising on either side of its entrance doorway. The upper storey still has an original medieval roof. The cloister was about 40m square and its eastern walk with eleven lierne-vaulted bays with buttresses between three-light windows forms the western part of the lower storey of the range. Three bays also remain of the southern walk which lay under the refectory and a shorter section survives of the northern alley. There is no evidence that this unusally large cloister had a western range, but it appears to have had a west porch.

COVENTRY   Warwickshire   *Franciscans*   SP 334787   To south of city centre

The Franciscans were established in Coventry by 1234 when Henry III allowed them to obtain shingles from royal woods at Coventry for covering their church. Ranulph de Blundeville, Earl of Chester was a major benefactor and his niece Cicely and her husband Roger de Montalt, who inherited Ranulph's possessions at Coventry, were both buried in the choir of the friary church. In 1269 Archbishop Peckham tried to settle a quarrel between the priory and the friary over lands obtained for the enlargement of the latter. In 1331 Edward III ordered various officials to facilitate the transportation of the body of the recently executed Roger, earl of March from the Franciscan church at Coventry to the parish church below the former earl's principal castle at Wigmore in Herefordshire. John Ward, first Mayor of Coventry was buried in the church here in 1348, as were several of his successors and various members of the Boteler, Spencer and Langley families, whilst the Hastings family had a chantry chapel on the north side. In 1378 Richard II allowed the friars to take stone from a quarry once held by his father at Cheylesmore and to create a postern gate through the adjacent city wall.

Provincial Chapters of the Franciscans were held in Coventry in 1420, 1472, 1489 and 1505. The Coventry Franciscans were noted for annually staging religious plays on the feast of Corpus Christi in which biblical history was presented in 42 acts, seven illustrating Old Testament scenes and the others the New Testament. A script of these, mostly dating from 1468, still survives. The scenes were presented on stages set on wheels drawn around the city and drew huge crowds. Margaret, Queen of Henry VI, attended in 1456, Richard III came in 1484, and Henry VII in 1492, the latter specifically "to see the plays acted by the Grey Friars". The friary was surrendered to Dr London by Warden John Stafford and ten friars in October 1538. The city corporation managed to save part of the friary church from destruction. All that now remains of it is a 14th century octagonal central tower and spire 66m high set upon two wide arches set on either side of a narrow cross passage of a type common in friary churches. One arch dates from 1830 and is now disfigured by the canopy of a modern cafe on the site of the former Christchurch of that period, which was bombed in 1940. The other arch now ignominiously overlooks the cafe waste-bins.

The Carmelite friary at Coventry

Franciscan friary tower at Coventry

DERBY   Derbyshire   *Dominicans*   SK 349365   On west side of town centre

Friar Gate and Friary Street are named after a Dominican house established c1230 in the parish of St Werburgh just outside the town defences, with Henry III as a generous benefactor. The precinct was eventually enlarged to over 16 acres. In 1344 the friary was attacked, some of its contents were taken and trees valued at £60 were cut down. Provincial chapters of the order were held here in 1310, 1346 and 1376, and Henry VI stayed at the friary in 1403. There were 26 friars here in 1323 but just six were left by 1534-5, others having recently fled abroad.

DONCASTER   South Yorkshire   *Carmelites*   SE 574032   On south side of town

This "right goodly house in the middle of town" was founded in 1350 by John and Maud Nicbrothere and Richard Euwere, although John of Gaunt, Duke of Lancaster was also an important benefactor. A provincial chapter was held here in 1376. Amongst several noted writers who belonged to this friary was Henry Parker, condemned for preaching on the poverty of Christ and His apostles and attacking secular clergy at Paul's Cross in 1464. Notables buried in the church here included Sir John Willis (executed by Edward IV in Doncaster in 1470 for his part in the Earl of Warwick's rebellion), and his wife Elizabeth, daughter of Lord Bemers, and also Margaret Cobham, wife of Ralph Neville, 2nd Earl of Northumberland, whose "goodly tomb of white marble" was later moved to the parish church. There were numerous bequests to "Our Lady of Doncaster" an image of the Virgin Mary said to cause miracles.

Here c1530 the friar John Bale taught "that Christ would dwell in no church made of stone and lime by man's hands, but only in heaven above and in man's heart on earth". During the Pilgrimage of Grace in 1535 the local lords occupied the friary whist negotiating with the rebel leader Robert Aske. Prior Lawrence Coke was imprisoned in the Tower of London for his part in the rebellion and condemned to death just before Cromwell himself fell from power in 1540. It is uncertain whether his pardon arrived in time to save his life. Prior Edward Stubbis and seven friars surrendered the house to Hugh Wyrrall and Tristham Teshe in November 1538. The image of the Virgin had already been removed on the order of the Archbishop of York. The friary had quite a lot of plate and had many tenements including an inn, although they were rather decayed.

DONCASTER   South Yorkshire   *Franciscan*   SE 571037   At NW end of the town

The earliest evidence of Franciscan friars here at the south end of an island formed by the Don and Cheswold rivers, reached from town by the Friars' Bridge, is in 1290, when the Pope granted an indulgence to those visiting their church. In 1291 Archbishop Romanus asked them to preach in support of a crusade at Doncaster, Blyth and Retford. Several royal grants for food in 1299, 1300 and 1301 suggest a compliment of 30 friars but the early part of Edward III's reign it varied from 18 to 27. Warden Thomas de Saundeby and four other friars were sued in 1332 for seizing and imprisoning John de Malghum. In 1335 Edward III pardoned the friars for having acquired land without permission during previous reigns upon which their church and houses had been built. Patrons buried in the friary church included Thomas, Lord Furnival, d1333, Sir Peter de Maulay, d1381, John Mauleverer, d1451, and Robert Skirley, d1522.

In November and December of 1536 Robert Aske, leader of the Pilgrimage of Grace, stayed in the friary with some of his followers whilst conferring with the royal commissioners lodged in the Carmelite friary. The house was surrendered Sir George Lawson in November 1538 by the warden and nine friars, three of whom were novices.

DONNINGTON   Berkshire   *Trinitarian*   Location Uncertain

Sir Richard Abberbury, who built the nearby castle in the 1380s has been claimed as being the founder of this house, which had an annual income of £20 when suppressed in 1538. Prior William Grainfelde is mentioned in 1404, and a will of 1500 included a bequest to the newly built Jesus Chapel added to the south side of the church.

DORCHESTER   Dorset   *Franciscan*   SY 695909   On north side of town

This friary on the river bank just east of the castle site now occupied by a prison is first mentioned in 1267, when the friars were taken to court for encroaching upon a road by having a wall constructed, during which a workman had fallen to his death. Richard III claimed the friary was a royal foundation and in 1483 granted it custody of the hospital of St John the Baptist, which would have provided some income from rents. However Henry VI had already granted the hospital to Eton College and the friars probably never had possession, although they had a small income from other tenements in the town. In 1485 they were given some valuable adjacent watermills by Sir John Byconil in return for various conditions, including the bringing of young boys into the friary who were to be known as Byconil's Friars, effectively losing their surnames in the process.

The friary was surrendered to the Bishop of Dover in September 1538 by the Warden William Germen and seven friars. The church furnishings included a small pair of organs, a set of canopied choir stalls, several tombs, a new tabernacle with a image of St Francis, three bells in the steeple, an assortment of clerical robes and vestments some blue velvet with embroidery. The chambers only contained two old carpets, a feather bed without a bolster, some bedding and meagre furnishings in the hall, refectory, buttery, kitchen and brewhouse, but there was some lead roofing on the steeple and cloister and there were "two horses belonging to the mill".

DROITWICH   Worcestershire   *Augustinian*   SO 895629   To SW of town centre

In 1331 Thomas Alleyn of Wyche was licensed to give the Austin friars a plot of land three hundred feet square for the building of a house and oratory, and the friars were given a further strips of adjoining land in 1343 and 1351, whilst the Bishop of Worcester left a bequest of ten marks in 1395. Letters patent issued in 1388 by Henry Duke, presumably then prior, refers to the founding of a cell for an anchorite on the south side of the church under patronage of Thomas Beauchamp, Earl of Warwick. This deed stipulates that any successors to the present anchorite, Henry de Stokebrugge, must come under the authority of the prior of the house and be Austin friars or at least wear their habit. In the 1530s the Bishop of Dover wrote to Thomas Cromwell to the effect that the buildings were in a poor state of repair, the only lead on the roofs being some guttering, and that the prior had disposed of any furnishings and assets of value.

The Franciscan friary at Dunwich

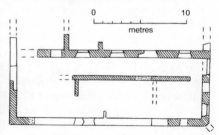

Plan of the Franciscan friary at Dunwich

DUNSTABLE   Bedfordshire   *Dominican*   TL 019217   Near the High Street

Excavations in 1988 found parts of the north walls of the nave and choir of the church with a possible central tower and a precinct wall closeby to the north which had to be moved further out when an aisle and porch were added to the nave in the 14th century. By the end of that period the choir only seems to have been used as a burial place. The friary was founded in 1259 at the instigation of Henry III and Queen Eleanor and local magnates but in the face of hostility from the canons of the priory who in 1287 obtained a nearby house as a means of preventing expansion of the friars' precinct without the consent of the priory. The friary may have survived until the early part of 1539, when the property was granted to one of the yeomen of the guard.

DUNWICH   Suffolk   *Dominincan*   Precise location unknown, now under the sea

The site of the friary founded in the mid 13th century by Sir Roger de Holish has been under the sea since at least 1754. A proposal in the 1380s for a move inland to Blythburgh 6km away never happened. Henry III donated oaks for building work in 1256. A boundary dispute with the Norwich Dominicans was eventually settled by adopting the county boundary between Norfolk and Suffolk, except that Rushmere and Mendham were to be regarded as within Dunwich's territory.

DUNWICH   Suffolk   *Franciscan*   TM 478704   To SE of the existing village

The surviving 14th century ruin, which at one time formed the core of an 18th century house, was a range along the south side of the southern of two cloisters, as suggested by a resistivity survey of the site, the church lying beyond the northern cloister. A cloister walk formed part of the lowest storey of the range, which retains several original windows, although none have any tracery remaining, and the upper walls are much patched and rebuilt. The spine wall of the range is thin and the south wall is reduced to its base. The precinct walls still mostly survive, although the cliff edge has now almost reached them on the east. On the west are two gateways almost side-by-side, one for carts and the other for pedestrians. The friary was founded in the mid 13th century by Richard and Alice FitzJohn with help from Henry III and appears to have moved inland to the present site after being given more land by the town corporation in 1289.

EASTON ROYAL   Wiltshire   *Trinitarian*   Near Easton church, 5km south of Pewsey

When the church of this friary founded in 1245 by Stephen de Tilsbury, Archdeacon of Wiltshire was demolished in 1590 a smaller new parish church had to be erected elsewhere and an effigy of Sir John Seymour, d1536 was moved to Great Bedwyn.

EXETER   Devon   *Dominican*   SX 922928   Within former east corner of city walls

Little appears to be known about the Dominican house here except that it was founded c1231-4. The Russells built a mansion called Bedford House on the site, replaced by Bedford Circus, itself succeeded by a shopping precinct after war-time bombing.

EXETER *   Devon   *Franciscan*   SX 921921   To SE of south corner of city walls

Excavations in the 1980s found parts of the south end of the dormitory range on the east (strictly speaking SE) side of the cloister with the reredorter at its outer (south) corner and evidence that the refectory range on the SW side of the cloister had been added later. The Franciscans moved here in the late 13th century from a more compact site near the priory of St Nicholas within the city walls.

GLOUCESTER   Gloucestershire   *Carmelites*   SO 835186   NE end of city centre

The bus station replacing a cattle-market of 1823 lies on the site of a Carmelite friary founded c1268 which lay just outside the North Gate. Queen Eleanor, Sir Thomas Giffard and Thomas, Lord Berkeley are credited as the founders. It was said to be a small house and had just three friars when surrendered in 1538, although there were 31 friars here in 1337. In 1343 they were allowed to acquire three and a half acres more land and in 1347 a better water supply was obtained through an agreement with the warden of the nearby hospital of St Bartholomew.

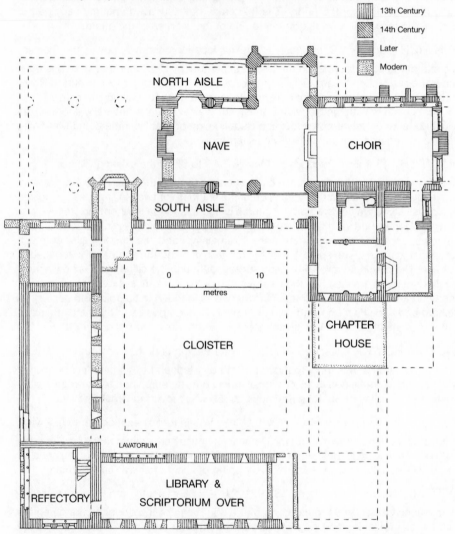

13th Century

14th Century

Later

Modern

NORTH AISLE

NAVE

CHOIR

SOUTH AISLE

0   10
metres

CHAPTER HOUSE

CLOISTER

LAVATORIUM

LIBRARY &
SCRIPTORIUM OVER

REFECTORY

Plan of the Dominican friary at Gloucester

GLOUCESTER   Gloucestershire   *Dominicans*   SO 829184   In western part of city

One of the most complete Dominican friaries left in England, this house was founded c1239 by Sir Simon de Hermshall on a site just within the south wall of the city that had once been an outer court of the castle. Henry III was a generous benefactor, donating oaks for nearly all the roofs, some of which still exist in over the church, where they have scissor-braced trusses below close-set collar-beams. The church was consecrated in 1284 and by then there were about 35 friars. Later on there were discipline problems, one friar in the 1330s discarding his habit to wander "as a vagabond".

After surrender by the prior and six friars in 1538 the friary was purchased by Alderman Thomas Bell, who was at times both Mayor and Sheriff of Gloucester. He made a mansion out of parts of the church comprising the west half of the 13th century choir, the crossing as remodelled in the 14th century with shallow transepts, and the eastern two bays of a six bay aisled nave still retaining one original 13th century arcade pier on each side. The later floors have been removed to re-open these spaces into one again. One original lancet remains in the choir north wall, which has 16th century buttresses. The north transept contained the staircase of Bell's mansion and has the outline of a large later window between set-back corner buttresses with canted angles.

Much of the east range including the chapter house has gone. However the much rebuilt west range containing the refectory with its pulpitum and triple south lancets, and the better preserved south range with an upper floor scriptorium or library, both survived because Bell used them as a factory for making hats and cloth. On the cloister side of the south range are remains of a lavatorium or washing place with six moulded trefoiled arches on shafts with moulded capitals. Also surviving is the prior's chamber, a creation of the late 15th century with an added oriel window in an unusual location in the north end of the east range next to the choir of the church where further original roofs survive along with old tiles and traces of wall paintings. The Bells used part of this area as a kitchen. The cloister was 24m square and had lean-to alleys of wood. Towards Blackfriars Lane parts of the medieval precinct wall still remain. The three later gateways incorporate reset medieval parts.

After Bell and his wife died in the 1560s the buildings passed to the Dennis family. In c1710, after they left, the house was subdivided and the other buildings were later used as workshops by stonemasons. Most of the 13th century features were only revealed after a restoration was begun in the 1960s by the Ministry of Works.

The Dominican friary at Gloucester from the west

The nave of the Franciscan friary at Gloucester

GLOUCESTER   Gloucestershire   *Franciscans*   SO 831084   In south part of city

The Franciscans were settled c1231 on a plot given by Thomas, Lord Berkeley which was soon extended southwards to the town wall. Not long afterwards Ralph of Maidstone resigned the bishopric of Hereford to join them. In 1246 Henry III allowed them to run a theology school within one of the towers of the town wall. The Black Prince managed to obtain a better water supply for them in 1357, after years of dispute with the Benedictine monks over the matter, and in 1365 they acquired more land.

The church was entirely rebuilt c1518 onwards by Maurice Berkeley, being described as "new builded" when surrendered by the last five friars (others had fled) in 1538 and it was subsequently adapted into several lodgings and a brewhouse, only to suffer damage in the siege of 1642. The cloister and choir had gone by 1721, and the East-gate market hall now lies over the site of the latter. All seven bays of the nave and its north aisle just as high and nearly as wide still survive in a very defaced condition, and with a house (now a library) of 1810 built into the western two bays. What remains of the arcade has lozenge-shaped piers. A double naved church such as this is unique for a friary church in England, although there are parallels in Ireland, Germany and France. The side windows with blind arcading below and between them were of four lights and the aisle east window had six lights, but not much remains of their tracery. The two facsimile shields on the south side towards the site of the cloister with arms of the Chandos and Clifford families date from when the ruin was consolidated in 1975-7.

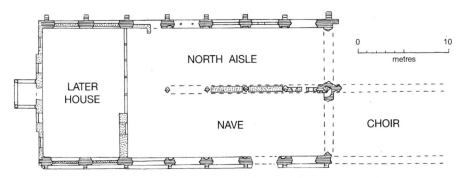

Plan of the Franciscan friary church at Gloucester

GORLESTON   Norfolk   *Augustinian*   TG 523049   North of the parish church

William and Margaret Woderove were buried in the church of this friary, which they founded c1300-05, and their son Roger gave the friars some more land in 1311. Richard de Clare and two late 14th century Pole earls of Suffolk were among other important benefactors buried here, where in later years Prior John Brome had a famous library. The friars also had a house in Ostend (corruption of Austin) Row in the town of Great Yarmouth which lies just across the river. The friary is said to have had quite a large church and was suppressed in 1538. Very minor remains of some friary buildings may survive between the houses of Burnet Lane and Beccles Road but nothing is now visible from either road.

GRANTHAM   Lincolnshire   *Franciscans*   SK 912359   North of the Market Place

The first mention of Franciscans here is in 1290, when Pope Nicholas IV granted an indulgence of one year and forty days of enjoined penance to those visiting their church on the feasts of the Virgin and those of St Francis, St Anthony and St Clare. The friary lay in the custody of Oxford and seems to have had twenty friars in 1300, when Bishop Dalderby licensed four of the friars to hear confessions. Four altars in the church and one in the infirmary chapel were dedicated by the same bishop in 1311. By then the earls of Surrey were giving the friars an annual grant of corn. In 1314 the Bishop of Durham allowed them to make a conduit to bring water into their house from a spring at Gonerby a kilometre to the west, which had been donated by Ralph of Barneby the previous year and was covered by an intake house until as recently as 1979. This supply now feeds the conduit dated 1597 in the market place of the town.

In 1339 and 1419 murderers took sanctuary in the church. On the latter occasion a bailiff took off the felons (the brasier Thomas Couper and the locksmith William Drusthorpe) to Lincoln but a jury insisted on their return to the friary. In 1492 a provincial chapter of the Premonstratensian order was held within the friary. Benefactors included Ralph Basset of Sapcote in 1377, Richard de Evingeham, Rector of Ewerby in 1397, Robert Wyntryingham, Canon of Lincoln in 1415, and Queen Catherine of Aragon. In 1513 her husband Henry VIII granted the friars a pardon for all kinds of transgressions or crimes which they might have committed before 1510. The Warden and other friars were later accused of using seditious language but were cleared when the matter was investigated by the Earl of Rutland at Thomas Cromwell's behest. The friary was surrendered in February 1539 to the Bishop of Dover, who reported that it was so poor that the king would receive only some lead, the bells and a chalice.

GREAT YARMOUTH   Norfolk   *Carmelites*   TG 522081   North end of town

This friary with a church dedicated to St Mary was founded by Edward I in 1276 and was entirely destroyed by fire in 1509, although friars remained here until their surrender to the Bishop of Dover in 1538. Little is known of their activities except that in 1378 they were allowed to close off a lane to make space for a extension of the buildings on the south side, provided that they created a new lane somewhere else.

GREAT YARMOUTH   Norfolk   *Dominicans*   TG 525068   South end of town

The founders of this friary established in 1267 were regarded as being Henry III, who in 1271 granted the friars a large square plot of land near the south gate, plus Godfrey Pilgrim, who built the church which was dedicated to St Dominic in 1280, and also Thomas Fastolf, who erected the domestic buildings about the same period, when 35 friars are recorded. The friary was flooded during a great storm 1287 but the earth bank begun soon afterwards to help protect it from further inundation was not allowed to be completed because it was said to be prejudicial to the town and its defences. The friary was never restored after being destroyed by fire in 1525, and it was surrendered to the Bishop of Dover in 1538.

GREAT YARMOUTH   Norfolk   *Franciscans*   TG 525072   In the middle of town

Hidden away within the The Rows, now in the custody of English Heritage, is a 14th century range incorporating the west cloister alley with two bays still covered with tierceron-star-vaults. West of the cloister is part of the outer wall of the south aisle of the nave with a pair of tomb recesses and some 14th century wall paintings discovered in the 1960s during clearance after wartime bomb damage. This aisle also had a porch.There was also a north aisle. The unusual feature of a crypt under the east end of the 55m long church was necessitated by the sloping site, which was expanded eastwards to Middlegate Street and west towards South Quay. The friary was probably founded c1226 by Sir William Gerbrigge. In 1302 the friars complained that local malefactors had broken down their fence next to the river. After surrender in 1538 to the Bishop of Dover the friary passed to Thomas Cromwell. He gave it to a nephew.

SOUTH AISLE

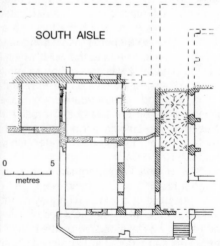

0   5
metres

The cloister of the Franciscan friary at Great Yarmouth   *Plan of the Franciscan friary at Great Yarmouth*

GREENWICH   Greater London   *Franciscans*   In the vicinity of the Queen's House.

The Observant Franciscans had obtained papal recognition as a separate order in 1415 but had no separate houses in England until 1481, when Edward IV founded a friary for them beside his manor-house at Greenwich. Initially the friars here seem to have used a small pre-existing chantry chapel of the Holy Cross, but after taking the throne in 1485 Henry VII enthusiastically supported the Observants in constructing a full set of new buildings here. Bequests at his death in 1509 included a large sum for this purpose to be held in trust by the Carthusian Prior of London, plus 100 marks left to each of five other Observant Franciscan houses. In 1502 the Greenwich friars seem to have been the main instigators behind the change of habits then adopted by the English Franciscans, which were henceforth to be the natural white-grey "as the sheep doth dye it", and consequently rather cheaper to obtain.

In 1498 Prince Edmund was christened in the friary church, and the probabilty is that the future Henry VIII was also christened in it in 1491, as were his daughters Mary and Elizabeth in 1516 and 1533. Henry's marriage to Catherine of Aragon in 1509 also probably took place here, the manor-house being enlarged into a palace. During the early part of Henry's reign the Observants were high in the royal favour. In 1513 the king commended them to the Pope for their poverty, sincerity, charity and devotion, whilst the queen is thought to have been admitted to the Franciscan Third Order, which included married lay people of both sexes. It appears that when staying in the palace she often rose early enough to be present in the friary church for the services of Matins and Lauds. In 1520 the celebrated scholar William Roy briefly lived here whilst he wrote the surviving Mountford Codex of the Greek text version of the New Testament, most probably at the instigation of Henry Standish, Bishop of St Asaph.

Not surprisingly the friars here mostly supported Queen Catherine and spoke out against Henry VIII's attempts to make himself head of the English church and divorce her. The Franciscan Provincial William Peto refused to depose the friary warden for preaching and making comments adverse to the kings interests and both were sent as prisoners to the Tower of London in June 1534. In August of that year all the Greenwich friars were expelled and sent off to confinement in other Franciscan houses, where some at least appear to have been kept in chains and probably half-starved as well since many of the 140 Observants confined during this period died in their cells. The survivors were still in confinement in March 1537. In May 1538 one of the most vociferous Greenwich friars, John Forrest, was burnt at a stake as a traitor and heretic whilst the Bishop of Worcester preached alongside the execution in favour of the king's position. By then the king had brought in less hostile ordinary Franciscans to occupy the Greenwich friary, and made the new community installed in March 1537 a gift of £100. They only lasted a year and a half before the friary was taken back into royal hands.

Because the premises were not quickly deposed of as was usual at the suppression of friaries it was possible for Queen Mary to revive the Franciscan community here in 1555 after the buildings had been repaired. She elevated the former Franciscan provincial William Peto to be her Bishop of Salisbury, and in March 1556 Cardinal Pole was constituted Archbishop of Canterbury in the friary church at Greenwich, just two days after Archbishop Cranmer had been burnt at a stake. The friars remained until Queen Elizabeth expelled them in February 1559, and most of them fled to the Netherlands. Old drawings show the layout of the 16th century palace, which was much favoured by Queen Elizabeth, of which all that now remains is a low undercroft which lay below its main hall, but nothing appears to be known about the buildings of the friary.

GRIMSBY   Lincolnshire   *Augustinians*   TA 269095   To north of old town centre

By 1300 Augustinian friars from Lincoln had built an oratory here without permission from the bishop. It lay on land which William Fraunk had given them and agreed to pay rents due for it to the king. The friars were allowed to acquire more land in 1305, and in 1315 Queen Isabella persuaded Edward II to allow them to acquire an adjacent messuage. Yet more land was acquired in 1319, 1333 and 1337, and in 1325 the bishop granted an indulgence to those visiting their church. In 1339 the friars and their attorney William Bray were granted a writ of protection for one year after some hostile townsfolk assaulted Friar Simon of Grimsby. They seem to have suffered a similar problem in the time of Henry VII. In October 1536 the prior gave financial support to the local rebellion but may have only done so to prevent the friary being burned. It was surrendered to the Bishop of Dover in February 1539, most of the friars having already fled abroad before Cromwell's agent John Freeman had visited it back in October. The bishop favoured the request by the mayor and aldermen that they should have the buildings in which to store ordnance and equipment for the defence of the town, but in August 1542 the five acre site was granted to the dean and chapter of Westminster Abbey.

GRIMSBY   Lincolnshire   *Franciscans*   TA 271096   To NE of the old town centre

This house was "sufficiently enlarged" in 1240-54, when William of Nottingham was the Franciscan provincial, so it must have existed in the 1230s. Henry III granted the friars twenty oaks from Sherwood Forest in 1255, and in 1305 Robert le Eyr relieved them of an annual rent due to the Knights Templars. Edward II pardoned the friars in 1313 for acquiring land without permission and allowed them to make an underground conduit to bring in water from Holm. In October 1536 the warden rode out to meet the local rebels and distributed to them some money borrowed from the prior of the Augustinian friars (see above). When John Freeman dissolved the house in October 1538 there were nine friars, although only six signed the surrender deed. The site by Garth Lane covered three acres. The bells and lead were said to be worth £80 to the king.

GUILDFORD   Surrey   *Dominicans*   SU 994496   At the west end of town centre

Edward I's mother Queen Eleanor founded this friary in 1275 in memory of her grandson Henry. Sir Hugh Fitz-Otho paid for the choir of the church, Lady Clarisan donated stalls for it, and John de Westpurle donated £100 and some timber towards the dormitory range. Edward II made an unsuccessful attempt to turn the house over to a group of seven Dominican nuns but the Pope turned the scheme down. Important later bequests came from wills of Richard Fitz-Alan, Earl of Arundel and Surrey dated 1393, and Sir Reginald Bray, dated 1503. When Henry IV and his family came to Guildford in February 1403 they stayed in the friary instead of the then very decayed apartments in the castle, and paid the friars compensation for damages and entertainment costs. Henry VIII built a himself a lodge in the friary grounds and payments were made to specific friars skilled in horticulture for help with laying out the lodge gardens. Here the king ratified a treaty with Scotland in 1534 in the presence of the Bishop of Winchester, the Duke of Norfolk, the Earl of Northumberland, Thomas Cromwell and others. Prior Cobden and six friars surrendered the friary to the Bishop of Dover in October 1538, just a year after the last royal visit, when they had been granted 20 marks per annum to help with repairs. Excavations in 1974-8 revealed that the church had a south aisle and a cloister to the north, the chapter house and sacristy being in the east range and the kitchen in the north range. Only the east part of the west range was revealed.

HARTLEPOOL   Durham   *Franciscans*   NZ 529338   North of St Hilda's church

This friary seems to have been founded before 1240 by the de Brus (Bruce) family and was surrendered in 1538 by a warden and 18 friars. Excavations in the 1980s revealed footings of the east end of the eight bay long choir. An aisle five bays long lay on the north side of the nave. To the south, but detached, lay the cloister. The 16th century house called The Friarage incorporates part of a friary building in its west wall.

In 1259 the Master of Sherburn Hospital bequeathed half a mark to some Dominicans in Hartlepool but there is no other evidence they had a community there.

HEREFORD   Herefordshire   *Dominicans*   SO 511405   To north of city walls

In Blackfriars Gardens in the angle between Widemarsh Street and Coningsby Steet is a 14th century preaching cross, the only one associated with a friary to remain in England. It is hexagonal with traceried openings and has a cross over its vaulted canopy. There is no entrance and it is too low for anyone to actually stand inside it. Nearby lies the 14th century west range which had the adjacent alley of the cloister recessed into its lower storey although the wall between the two parts has gone. Some original buttresses and windows survive, along with later windows and fireplaces, and a projecting stair-turret of the early 17th century when Sir Thomas Coningsby lived here. It is said to have suffered some damage during the Civil War period, the location being just outside the city walls and for while until restoration in the 1850s was used as a stable. This friary was founded c1276. Edward III and the Black Prince and several bishops attended the consecration of the church in the mid 14th century.

HEREFORD   Herefordshire   *Franciscans*   SO 507398   To west of city walls

Little appears to be known about this friary, except that Owen Tudor, grandfather of Henry VII, was buried in a chapel forming part of the friary church after capture and execution by Edward IV in 1461 after his victory at Mortimer's Cross.

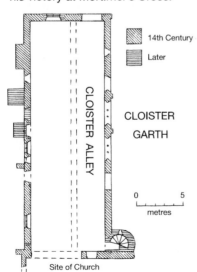

14th Century

Later

CLOISTER ALLEY

CLOISTER GARTH

0   5
metres

Site of Church

Plan of Hereford friary remains

Inside of the north range of the Dominican friary at Hereford

Old print of Hitchin Friary

HERTFORD Hertfordshire *Trinitarians* TL 328127 At the east end of the town

In 1261 Trinitarian friars took over a much older hospital of St Mary Magdalene just outside the town and removed the lepers. It is thought to have been dissolved early in Henry VIII's reign. A Catholic church stands on or near to the site.

HITCHIN Hertfordshire *Carmelites* TL 184288 To south of the parish church

This friary was founded in 1317 by Edward II and was given more land in 1351 by John de Cobham, the site being beside the east bank of the River Hiz. Henry VIII gave the friars 40s in 1530. Immediately after the prior and four priors surrendered the friary in October 1538 the church and steeple were knocked down. However parts of the cloister on the north side of the church still remain in the mansion created out of the rest by the Radcliffe family. Four arches remain of the north cloister walk and two more probably of 15th century date on the west, where there are three small cusped single light windows and a pair of mullioned 16th century windows of brick. The house also has good facades of the 1670s and the 1770s, the latter designed by Robert Adam.

HOUNSLOW Middlesex *Trinitarians* SU 112747 2km SW of the town centre

The hospital by the River Crane just above Baber bridge which is first mentioned c1200 seems to have been given about fifty years later to the Trinitarian friars by Henry III's brother Richard, Earl of Cornwall. Edward III often passed by when travelling between Westminster and Windsor. He was a generous benefactor to these friars, who provided a chaplain for a royal lodging built on their land at Hatton Grange in 1376 which was to revert to the friars on the king's death. The friars also provided a warden for a hospital at Crediton and a chaplain for Warland, near Totnes, both in far away Devon. This was the richest of England's friaries, holding 80 acres beside the river and on Hounslow Heath and total endowments worth £74 per annum in 1535, and it seems to have been the residence of the provincial of the Trinitarians. Parts of the friary remained in use as a manor house and parish church until demolished and replaced by a new church of Holy Trinity in 1828, in which is one monument with kneeling figures of c1540 facing each other saved from the old church.

HULL   East Yorkshire   *Augustinians*   TA 100286   Near Holy Trinity Church

Austin friars from York established a new friary here in 1317 on a plot of land 205ft long by 115ft wide given by Geoffrey de Hotham and John de Wetwang. One of those who condemned Wycliffe's teaching in 1382 was the Cambridge scholar Friar John de Homyngton, who had been allowed by the prior general to take up residence here and take one of the other friars as his servant. In 1381 Richard II had given him a writ of protection for himself, his servant, chamber, books and goods, since there were envious persons scheming to expel him. There are said to have been eighteen friars here in the late 15th century, all entirely dependent on alms. In 1520 the mariner Richard Wilflet endowed the lights on the altars of St Mary and St Catherine in the friary church.

This house survived as late as March 1539 when it was finally surrendered by Prior Alexander Ingram to the Bishop of Dover. Excavations in 1994 and 1999 revealed footings of the church and evidence of the original temporary timber-framed buildings. Also found were 245 skeletons, some of which gave clear evidence of syphillis being rife in medieval Hull. Burial garments including women's girdles were unusually well preserved, as were the 14th century wooden coffins. Burials after the late 14th century were in shrouds, taking up less space. The layout of the friars' medieval garden was also preserved, it and the house having remained in use until the mid 17th century.

HULL   East Yorkshire   *Carmelites*   TA 102288   East side of old town centre

Carmelite tradition maintains this friary was founded in 1290 by Edward I, Sir Robert Ughtred and Sir Richard de la Pole. There appear to have been 13 friars in 1298 but their numbers increased rapidly and many townsfolk attended their services, so that Edward I in 1304 gave them a much larger new three acre site outside the town walls in exchange for the original modest site.

A new church was begun in 1307, after Pope Clement V ratified the move, and it was complete enough for it to be consecrated in 1311. Further land was obtained in 1320 and another acre and a half was given by the Pole family in 1352. Bequests by women to the image of the Virgin in the church were common and in 1523 Dame Joan Thutescrosse left £4 towards rebuilding work on the church. There were eight friars in the 1530s, and in March 1539 Prior John Wade surrendered the house to the Bishop of Dover.

The prior's tower house at Hulne from the SE

A distant view of the ruins of the Carmelite friary at Hulne

HULNE   Northumberland   *Carmelite*   *NU 163157*   In park 2.5km NW of Alnwick

Founded in 1242 by William de Vesci, Lord of Alnwick, Hulne was one of the two earliest Carmelite houses in England. Despite the loss of the north walls of the church, the cloister garth walls, most of the west range and the south side of the refectory range on the south it retains the most complete layout of a medieval Carmelite friary in England. The parts that do survive in ruins largely retain their medieval features and character, and appear to be all of c1250-90, the only later alterations being some 16th or 17th century features in the south range, which was converted to domestic use, and the insertion in 1778 of a summer house across part of the site of the west range.

Surrounding the ruins is the original 15th century precinct wall with a square gatehouse on the south side with a vaulted entrance passage flanked by a porter's room. This complete precinct wall is a rare survival and little altered except for new gateways of 1778 facing east and SW. The wall is 3.6m high and has blocked secondary gateways facing west and north. All around the SW corner there are remains of workshops, stores and guest rooms, whilst in the middle of the west side, dominating the site, is an embattled tower house built in 1486 by Sir Henry Percy (according to a reset slab now inside) presumably to provide the prior with defensible accommodation (see photos on page 51). The tower has an entrance with an adjoining straight staircase on the north, two turrets on the western corners and another turret running the full width at the east end. The two levels over the vaulted basement were thrown into one by removing a floor in the 1770s and then linked by a bridge to the summer house.

On the south side of the precinct, near the main gateway, is the infirmary, a late 13th century building now converted into a private house. The chapel forming the east part has an original east window with plate-tracery, whilst the hall in the west part has a three-light window with intersecting tracery and several modern windows. Parts of the 2.7m high wall of an outer precinct remain to the NE.

The church lies on the north side of a cloister court 24m square. It had a nave and chancel of equal length divided by two crosswalls (known only from excavation) creating a walking space between the two parts, perhaps the earliest example of this layout in England. The nave has three cusped lancets set high up on the south and contains a memorial slab with a tau-cross pierced by three nails. Another old slab now lies in the summer-house and a third, brought in from Alnmouth, is fixed to the nave west wall in which is a lancet and a vesica above. There were rooms to the west of here, a rather unusual feature. Because of the friary's rural location it was never necessary to add an aisle to the nave to accommodate more layfolk. The choir retains triple stepped sedilia, a piscina and windows with twinned lancets with a circle between the heads in the south wall. Only the lower parts remain of the east wall and its large window. A doorway by the sedilia leads through to a two storey sacristy with several lancet windows and a piscina.

On the east and west sides of the cloister the walkways formed nearly half of the width of the lower storey of the ranges, whilst the walkways on the north and south had lean-to roofs against the nave and refectory. A wide doorway on the east side led though an ante-room (now lacking its sidewalls) through to the chapter house, which projects entirely beyond the range and has four trefoiled lancets on the south side and remains of a five-light east window.. The dayroom south of the chapter house anteroom has a later fireplace on the east side. The dormitory lay above here, and extending east from the SE corner is a narrow range which contained the reredorter beyond a narrow warming-house with a fireplace in a breast projecting on the south side.

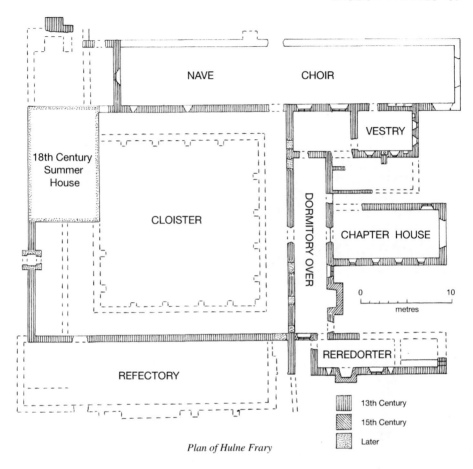

NAVE

CHOIR

VESTRY

18th Century Summer House

CLOISTER

DORMITORY OVER

CHAPTER HOUSE

0   10
metres

REREDORTER

REFECTORY

13th Century

15th Century

Later

Plan of Hulne Frary

Hulne Friary from the NE

Parish church of Holy Trinity at Ingham

HUNTINGDON   Cambridgeshire   *Augustinian*   TL 237720   NW end of town

The first mention of the friary is in 1286, when Edward I donated eight oaks towards building works. In 1335 the friars were pardoned for acquiring more land without a royal licence, and in 1354 they were in trouble for forcibly taking a man about to be hung off to sanctuary in St Andrew's church. In 1363 they were allowed to make a water conduit through the town. The house was surrendered to the Bishop of Dover in 1538.

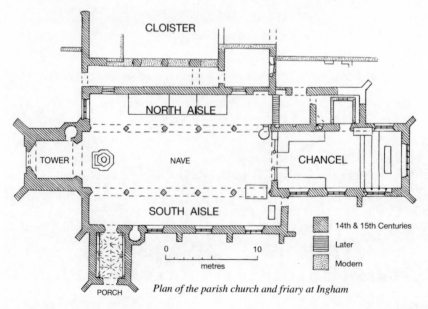

Plan of the parish church and friary at Ingham

ILCHESTER   Somerset   *Dominicans*   Location Uncertain

In 1263 permission was granted for land in Ilchester to be granted to the Dominicans for founding a friary next to the gaol. The friars were allowed to purchase an adjacent messuage in 1271, and in 1283 to enclose another two and a half acres. Still more land was obtained in 1350. The trader William Balsham was buried in the church in 1444.

INGHAM   Norfolk   *Trinitarians*   TG 391260   2km NE of Stalham, east Norfolk

A new replica brass in the parish church of the Holy Trinity shows Sir Miles Stapleton, d1364, and his wife holding hands and there are indents and fragments of other brasses of their descendants. In 1360 Sir Miles had brought in Trinitarian friars to serve the church, the chancel of which had been rebuilt c1340 by Sir Oliver de Ingham, whose fine but mutilated tomb lies on the north side. The chancel has a good set of sedilia on the south side, a five-light east window, three-light side windows and contains a set of medieval stalls, now rebuilt without their misericords. A tiny modern vestry lies within the ruins of a medieval one with a spiral stair in one corner to an upper storey.

When founded the community had just three members although thirteen were intended, led by a prior and a sacrist. The latter was responsible for looking after the parishioners interests and possibly used the two upper levels of rooms over the tierceron-vaulted south porch as a residence, since the late 14th century aisled nave with five bay arcades remained in use by parishioners. It contains another tomb chest with defaced effigies of a late 14th century knight and wife of the de Bois family and has a west tower with double-stepped battlements, flushwork on the buttresses, and a four light west window, an arrangement more typical of an ordinary parish church.

The north aisle was extended eastwards to provide a two chapels, one above the other and both now ruined, between the aisle and the vestry. Two doorways led from the aisle into the surviving south alley of the cloister to the north. The other buildings have vanished and even the ground on which they stood has been quarried away. The upper doorway in the aisle must have led through to the dormitory in the east range.

In 1492 the four professed brethren and two unprofessed brethren were quite severely examined by the local archdeacon on behalf of the bishop but no fault could be found. The house was sold to William Woodhouse in 1536 by the community and this was upheld in court on the grounds that because it was a house of crossed friars rather than monks or canons it was not liable for suppression at that time.

Choir stalls at Ingham

Remains of cloister alley at Ingham

IPSWICH   Suffolk   *Carmelites*   TM 163445   South side of town centre

Carmelites arrived here from Norwich in 1278 probably as a result of the provincial chapter there in that year. They obtained more land in 1297, and 1321 when buildings were begun, and again in 1344 and 1996, creating a plot extending from St Stephen's Lane to Queen Street on the south side of the Butter Market. Provincial chapters of the order were held here in 1300 and 1312, on each occasion the prior of the house being elected as provincial of the order. This friary was one of the largest Carmelite houses and had a number of noted scholars including John Polsted, author of twenty religious tracts, and John Pascall who became Bishop of Scutari in 1344 and served three years as a suffragan bishop in the diocese of Norwich before being translated to the see of Llandaff. The church was rebuilt in the late 15th century, being consecrated in 1477 by Thomas Bradley, Bishop of Dromore in the province of Ulster, himself a friar. John Bale, Bishop of Ossory (Kilkenny) 1553-63 was prior here 1533-36 and although he later married and became a zealous Protestant he evidently respected what the Carmelites had taught him since he was less harsh in his criticism of them than of other religious orders. The friary was surrendered to the Bishop of Dover in November 1538.

IPSWICH   Suffolk   *Dominicans*   TM 166443   To SE of Town Centre

This friary was founded in 1263 by Henry III, who purchased land to donate to it in that year and again in 1265. By 1278 it had as many as 50 friars. In 1275 a commission had been sent to look at whether the friars should be allowed to extend a proposed block between their dormitory and the town dyke. The house was further enlarged in 1308 and 1334 and the townsfolk contributed more land in 1348. The resulting plot eventually extended between the churches of St Margaret and St Mary at Quay. The friary was surrendered in November 1538 to the Bishop of Dover and granted to the corporation. Part was demolished and rest used as Christ's Hospital almshouses.

Following on from excavations in 1983 when part of the refectory was located, and redevelopment of the site, the lower parts of the church and chapter house are now laid out in a garden between rows of flats between Foundation Street and Lower Orwell Street to the south of Tacket Street. The church was 55m long and had an aisled nave of six bays, separated by a walking space from a choir with a chantry chapel on the south side, towards the construction of which the Duke of Suffolk left a large bequest. The east wall of the sacristy beside the choir still stands high with an irregular arcade or four pointed arches and beyond it is the east end of the chapter house. There appear to have been two cloisters extending south of the nave with just a single wall between them. It was the southern cloister buildings that became almshouses.

IPSWICH   Suffolk   *Franciscans*   TM 161442   To south of town centre

Now moved to the Greyfriars Concourse nearby is the last remaining fragment of this friary in the parish of St Nicholas. It has a triple lancet with a transom unusually going across at the springing of the arch. The friary was founded in 1298 by Sir Robert and Ursula Tiptot of Nettlestead who were buried in the church, and was given more land in 1332. Also buried here were several other Tiptots and members of the Spenser, de Vere and Ufford families. Just before the house was suppressed late in 1538 Lord Wentworth of Nettlestead told Thomas Cromwell that the townsfolk had given so litle to the friars of late that they had been forced to dispose of some of their property in order to find money for food.

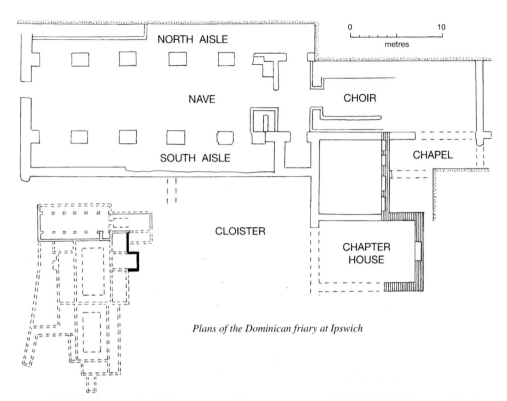

0   10
metres

NORTH AISLE

NAVE

CHOIR

SOUTH AISLE

CHAPEL

CLOISTER

CHAPTER
HOUSE

Plans of the Dominican friary at Ipswich

Remains of the Dominican friary at Ipswich

KILDALE   North Yorkshire   *Crutched Friars*   Location Unknown

Edward II pardoned Sir Arnold de Pary for giving the Crutched friars here a messuage and ten acres of land. In 1312 the friars were denounced and placed under an interdict by Archbishop Greenfield for celebrating divine service without his permission. The community may not have survived much longer and nothing further is known of it.

KINGS LANGLEY   Hertfordshire   *Dominican*   TL 064030   West of the village.

Edward II founded this friary beside his royal palace as a result of a vow made in 1308. John de Wareford, a member of his household, became its first prior. More endowment was provided by the king in 1311 to sustain another fifteen friars here, giving a total of 45, although a hundred may have been envisaged at one time. In 1312 the king gave 700 marks towards work on the church, allowing it to be consecrated that summer. The royal favourite Piers Gaveston was buried here in 1314 after being killed by jealous nobles, the funeral being attended by the Archbishop of Canterbury and four other bishops. In 1315 Prior John became the king's confessor. Edward III donated fishing rights to the friary in 1358 and other gifts later. Back in 1349 he had founded a house of Dominican nuns at Dartford in Kent as a means of providing the King's Langley house with a regular income without it actually owning lands on which rents were due. By 1356 the nuns were holding properties worth £300 a year (see page 112). In 1400 the body of the deposed and recently murdered Richard II was buried at the friary at Kings Langley, but Henry V later had the body moved to Westminster Abbey. Now transferred to the parish church is the late 14th century tomb of Edmund of Langley, Duke of York, and his wife, who was a daughter of Peter, King of Castile. In 1557 Queen Mary brought in seven nuns from the former Dartford nunnery to take over the friary, but the first parliament called by Queen Elizabeth declared void all restorations of monastic houses since the death of Edward VI. One 14th century domestic range with a crown-post roof and several original windows and doorways still survives aligned north-south within buildings begun c1900 of what is now a Rudolf Steiner school, and a minor fragment of the south wall of the choir some distance to the south is incorporated in a boundary wall. Richard Ingworth, the suffragen Bishop of Dover entrusted by Henry VIII with suppressing the friaries in 1538 had been a former prior of this house.

The surviving range of the friary at Kings Langley

Gateway of the Augustinian friary at King's Lynn

Gateway of the Carmelite friary at King's Lynn

KINGS LYNN   Norfolk

Augustinian   TF 618205   N of town centre

The Augustinians are thought to have arrived here in the 1270s. They were given more land in 1295, 1306, 1311, 1329 and 1338. Five tenements were added to the site in 1364 and in 1383 the Bishop of Norwich give the friars a spring and allowed them to take a conduit from it through his land over to their friary. One of the earliest accounts of the history of England in the English language was written here by Prior John Capgrave, d1467. Kings Henry V, Henry VI and Henry VII all stayed in the friary when visiting King's Lynn. Thomas Potter was prior in 1535 when the friars are recorded as having three tenements in the town worth 26s. 8d per annum. Prior William Wilson and ten other friars surrendered the friary in September 1538. A modest and rather patched 15th century gateway arch survives in a boundary wall beside Austin Street.

KINGS LYNN   Norfolk   *Carmelites*   TF 620195   South end of town centre

Lord Bardolph is said to have founded this friary near the River Lynn, which is first mentioned in 1261 with regard to the friars closing off a lane. In 1277 Edward I gave them six oaks and in 1285 allowed them to extend their churchyard across a former lane, provided that they created another public lane further north. A later Lord Bardolph was buried in the church in 1386 and the Hastings family were also major benefactors. The friary was surrendered by Prior Robert Newman and ten other friars in September 1538. A late 14th century brick gateway remains at the south end of Bridge Street.

KINGS LYNN   Norfolk   *Dominican*   TF 620199   East side of town centre

By the early 1270s this friary between Clow Lane and Skinner Lane had 40 friars, and there were 45 in the 1320s. A water supply was brought in from near Middleton, almost four miles away. Provincial chapters of the order were held here in 1304, 1344 and 1365. The buildings were damaged by fire c1456 and the friars were still struggling to repair them twenty years later. Only two friars signed the surrender deed in 1538, the day and month of which were never filled in.

Model of the Franciscan friary at King's Lynn

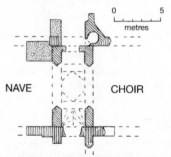

Franciscan friary at King's Lynn:
plan of the central tower

Tower of the Franciscan friary at King's Lynn

Franciscan friary at King's Lynn:
plan of the central tower

KINGS LYNN   Norfolk   *Franciscan*   TF 620198   East side of town centre

A slender and delightful late 14th century hexagonal central tower of brick with stone dressings still remains in a public garden between St James Street and Millfleet. The tower stands on a vaulted cross passage set into the 13th century church, of which the west end of the 26m long choir still remains with jambs of the first windows on either side. The tower has stepped corner buttreses, two tiers of windows with transoms, a traceried parapet and a semi-octagonal staircase turret, and leans one degree out of vertical in the course of 28m of height. The friary is thought to have been founded in the 1230s and was enlarged in 1300, the site eventually extending to Tower Place, London Road and Greyfriars Road. Beside the ruin is a brass model suggesting how the complete layout of buildings may have looked.

KINGS LYNN   Norfolk   *Friars of the Sack*   Location Unknown

When the Friars of the Sack were suppressed in England in 1317 and the last few members obliged to join one of the houses of the other four chief orders, Robert Flegg, prior of their house in King's Lynn, was provincial of their order in England.

KNARESBOROUGH W. Yorkshire *Trinitarians* SE 351564 South of town centre

Richard, Earl of Cornwall seems to have introduced Trinitarian friars in the 1240s to take over the chapel and hermitage founded in the 1190s by Robert Flower. Robert had been canonised by 1252, when Pope Innocent IV granted an indulgence to those who helped to complete the monastery, and in 1255 Henry III contributed three oaks to the friars. In 1276 Edmund, Earl of Cornwall allowed them to build a watermill beside the adjacent River Nidd. In 1311 the minister here was summoned to a provincial council which was involved in the trial of the recently suppressed Knights Templar. The priory was destroyed by the Scots during Robert Bruce's invasion of Yorkshire in May 1318 but Edward II and Edward III did what they could to support the subsequent rebuilding, the friars eventually being allowed to appropriate several local churches.

In 1366 Archbishop Thoresby tried to patch up the poor relations between the English minister of the order and the brethren at Knaresborough and ordered "that in future the cloister and dormitory should be kept free from the invasion of secular persons, and especially women of doubtful character, both by day and night".

In the 1380s, when William de Pudsey was provincial prior, a settlement was made for his retirement at Knaresborough, where he had been minister. He was to have a well furnished and heated chamber and a servant, and to be excused from choir duties and to be answerable only to his successor as provincial head. He was briefly deposed from office, but the pope re-instated him in 1402. That year Boniface IX authorised the minister and six other priests at Knaresborough to hear confessions from those that visited their church on the feasts of Holy Trinity and St Peter and St Paul. The pope also then allowed the English Trinitarian friars to admit boys under the age of twenty to their houses and to drop the portion of revenues assigned for bringing back captives from the Holy Land below the one third originally ordained. He also granted an indulgence of three years and forty days to those helping support the friars at Knaresborough. There is a mention of sisters as well as brethren in 1411, presumably laywomen rather than nuns. A book of this era from the friary survives in Trinity College, Cambridge.

In the 1450s the friars made a stone conduit to carry water to the friary from the Dropping Well in the Little Park, although the system later fell into disrepair. In 1536 one of the friars, Robert Ashton, was one of the organisers of the Pilgrimage of Grace, after which he escaped to Scotland. The minister remained loyal to the crown and was involved in the trial and execution of two rebels in York. Minister Thomas Kent and nine other priests surrendered their house at the very end of December 1538, and the pensions they were granted took nearly two thirds of the annual value reckoned at £93.

There are no remains of the friary itself, which stood by Abbey Road, just below where the Chapel of Our Lady of the Crag, a still functioning shrine founded in 1409, is cut into the sandstone cliff, complete with an altar, blank arcading and vaulting all carved out of the native rock. Possibly it was served by the friars at one time.

LANCASTER Lancashire *Dominicans* SD 479616 In middle of city centre

Sir Hugh Harrington founded the friary c1260. The friars were asked in 1291 by the Archbishop of York to preach in Lancaster, Kendal and (Kirkby) Lonsdale in favour of a new crusade, and in 1311 and c1320 they were given more land. There is a mention of a chantry in the friary church which had been founded by the ancestors of Sir Thomas Lawrence of Ashton. The friary was surrendered to the king in 1539. Excavations near Dalton Square in 1982 found parts of the 13th century south range with 100 original mosaic floor-tiles. This part was probably the refectory.

LEICESTER   Leicestershire   *Augustinians*   SK 582048   To west of city centre

This friary is first mentioned in 1304 when Thomas, Earl of Lancaster obtained a licence to donate three messuages for enlarging it, but Simon de Montfort, Earl of Leicester is thought to have been the original founder back in the 1250s. The friary church of St Catherine is mentioned as under construction in 1306. Two cloisters extended in line to the north of it. A general chapter of the order was held here in 1376. About that time Thomas Ratcliffe was a renowned preacher here. The friary and other small properties in the town were surrendered in November 1538 by the prior and three friars.

LEICESTER   Leicestershire   *Dominicans*   SK 577047   To NW of city centre

The friary stood on an island in the River Soar and is first mentioned in 1284. It is assumed to have been founded by Simon de Montfort, Earl of Leicester or his successor during Henry III's reign. Initially the friars seem to have used the parish church of St Clement for their services but this arrangement proved unsatisfactory and eventually they built their own church. Early in Edward III's reign there appear to have been 30 friars. Henry VII donated oaks for rebuilding the dormitory in 1487. The friary was surrendered by the prior and nine friars in November 1538.

LEICESTER   Leicestershire   *Franciscans*   SK 586042   South of the city centre

In 1402 eight friars and a master of divinity of this friary founded c1230 were arrested and taken to London for trial for continuing to support the cause of the deposed and murdered Richard II. Two other friars managed to escape being arrested. It took three trials before different juries before they were found guilty and executed. When a general chapter of the order was held here later in 1402 speaking against Henry IV was forbidden. Richard III was buried here after being killed in the battle of Bosworth in 1485. The friary was surrendered in 1538 by the warden and six friars.

LEICESTER   Leicestershire   *Friars of the Sack*   Location unknown

In 1295 Bishop Sutton forbad the conversion of the site formerly occupied by the Friars of the Sack in Leicester to secular use. There are no other references to them.

The surviving parts of the Franciscan friary at Lichfield

Range of the Franciscan friary at Lincoln

LEWES Sussex *Franciscans* TQ 418102 East of the bus station in town centre

Most of the site was levelled or destroyed in the late 19th and early 20th century but excavations have found slight traces of walls of the church beside the High Street and evidence of a cloister to the south. The friary existed by 1249 when a thief took sanctuary in the church. There were 24 friars here in 1299. When the friary was surrendered at the end of 1538 the value of the goods here did not cover the community's debts.

LICHFIELD Staffordshire *Franciscan* SK 116094 West of town centre

The Franciscans had a chapel and house under construction here by 1237, when Henry III donated them ten oaks. Probably Alexander Stevensby, Bishop of Coventry and Lichfield was the founder, this being a local tradition perpetuated by John Leland. In 1241 the sheriff was authorised "to clothe the friars minor of Lichfield". The friary was destroyed along with much of the town by fire in 1291, and in 1294 the 60 marks handed over by the monks of Westminster in settlement of a dispute with the Franciscans was split between the friaries of Lichfield and Winchelsea then both being rebuilt.

In 1310 the friars were granted a new water supply to the SW of the city and empowered to build a conduit and supply pipes to the friary. In c1325 two of the friars were attacked and beaten whilst on their way to Newport, and c1338 another group on the way to Worcester were attacked and the novice with them was abducted and stripped of his habit. The friars acquired another two acres of land in 1329 and the masses they were commissioned to say for the relatives and friends of Philip de Turvill, d1337 in his will added another £10 per annum to their income. The many bequests to the friary included £20 from Catherine, Countess of Warwick in 1369, and four books in 1498 from Richard Martin, a suffragan bishop to the Archbishop of Canterbury.

In 1531 Warden Richard Mason and one of the other friars were rebuked by the cathedral chapter for the preaching of a sermon which the townsfolk interpreted as an attack on the system of tithes and oblations. The chapter also ordered the removal of seats from the nave of the friars' church to make attendance there by laymen at the services less attractive. With some reluctance Richard Mason, who was said to be "hideously disfigured in the face by a skin disease" surrendered the friary to the Bishop of Dover in August 1538. The warden was paid a pension until his death in 1558, even though his friary had been "more in debt than all the stuff in it will pay". The debts included rent due to the bishop and money borrowed for recent repairs to the choir. Purchasers of parts of the friary had to agree to take the materials within three years.

From excavations in 1933 we know that the church was about 60m long and had an aisled nave of five bays. Separated from its south side by a narrow court was the main cloister which was 24m square. Immediately east of it, and south of the choir, lay a second cloister about 16m square, on the east side of which was the chapter house, whilst the infirmary lay along its south side with the new and old guest houses extending further south from it. Friary Road built in the 1920s now cuts across where these guest houses and the refectory south of the main cloister once lay. West of the refectory was the buttery with the kitchen south of it. The surviving much altered range on the south side of the road became a mansion. It was occupied by the Duke of Cumberland during his campaign against the Jacobites in 1745, was later used as a school, and now houses the public library. The old part seems to have originally contained apartments for officials and appears to be late 15th or early 16th century. Adjoining the building is a late 13th century coffin lid of a local merchant called Richard, evidence that laymen were buried in the friary precincts as early as that.

LINCOLN   Lincolnshire   *Augustinian*   SK 977722   To the north of the cathedral

John Leland recorded the ruins of the Augustinian friary as being on the south side of the suburb outside the Newport Gate. The friars settled here c1270 and in 1291 were licensed to have their church and precinct consecrated. Despite having sent some of their number off to found a new house in Grimsby in 1293 there were thirty friars here in 1300, and as many as 36 in 1335. Provincial chapters of the order were held here in 1307 and in 1332. At the time of its surrender to the Bishop of Dover in February 1539 the friary covered about four acres.

LINCOLN   Lincolnshire   *Carmelites*   SK 973708   To SW of railway station.

Henry III granted the Carmelites six beech trees for a kiln in 1269 and the friary is said to have been founded in that year by Odo of Kilkenny. In 1280 Edward I allowed the addition of more land. It appears that a provincial chapter was held here in 1287 at which it was agreed to adopt the white capes from which the Carmelites became known as the White Friars. There were 28 friars in 1300 and this had risen to 34 in 1335. Peter Raymond, Prior General of the whole order of the Carmelites was present at another provincial chapter held here in 1343. John Leland says that the friary once had a fine library including books about the life of St Edward the Confessor and Roman histories of Eutropius and Paulus Diaconus. When surrendered to the Bishop of Dover in February 1539 the friary had little of value except the lead on its roofs. The site, bounded by the High Street to the east and the river to the west, covered four acres and was later used for railway purposes. Excavations in the 1980s before a retail complex was built over it revealed part of the buttressed north wall of a 15th century outbuilding.

LINCOLN   Lincolnshire   *Dominicans*   SK 981719   To the east of the cathedral

The Dominicans were settled in the suburb of Silvergate outside Pottergate by 1238, when Henry III gave them 100s towards the expenses of hosting a provincial chapter here. He gave £10 towards a second provincial chapter in 1244 and ten oaks towards building work in 1255. The friars obtained a spring within lands of a cell of St Mary's Abbey at York in 1260 and were allowed to make a water conduit along the road from it to the friary. Lands donated at various times eventually amounted to about ten acres.

Edward I donated funds for provincial chapters here in 1293 and 1300, and gave the friars some oaks in 1284 and 1290 towards work on the church. It was consecrated along with the Lady Chapel in 1311. Here in 1320 was buried a major benefactor, Walter Jorse, Archbishop of Armagh, a former friar. Some of the local parish priests were against the friars hearing confessions and in 1300 Bishop Dalderby refused to licence as penitentiaries all 21 friars from this house presented by the provincial prior. In 1314 the prior of Lincoln was one of the eight officials deposed by the provincial chapter at London. Other provincial chapters were held at Lincoln in 1325 and 1388. The number of friars dramatically rose from 38 in 1328 to 48 in 1335.

In 1345 friar John of Lincoln failed to be elected to the see of St Asaph and afterwards required protection from people offended whilst he was acting as confessor to John de Warenne, Earl of Surrey. In 1390 the Prior General acquitted John Muren of a theft at the Derby friary and sent him to occupy a recently built chamber in the Lincoln friary, where he was to be master of students. Richard of Helmsley was appointed a lecturer to the students at the same time, the prior being warned not to impede him in his duties. When surrendered to the Bishop of Dover in February 1539 the friary was described as being poor but with the buildings' roofs all well-leaded.

LINCOLN   Lincolnshire   *Franciscans*   SK 977714   To east of lower part of town

Early in 1231 Henry III confirmed a grant by the citizens of Lincoln to the Franciscans of land by the guildhall which had been made available by the sub-dean, William of Beningworth. In 1237 the friars obtained the guildhall itself, the townsfolk being given another place for a guildhall by the king, who in 1258 allowed the friars to block a postern in the city wall and to erect buildings over the lane that had led to it. The resulting four acre site was thus bounded by the city wall on the east, the river on the south and by Silver Street and Free School Lane on the north and west. Timber for building the church was donated by Edward In 1284. Access by the townsfolk to the city wall remained an issue, resulting in a complaint by the friars about broken enclosures in 1321, when they also got the king to insist on their charters being returned.

Provincial chapters were held here in 1288, 1293 and 1295. It appears that there were 53 friars here in 1300, although this had dropped to 37 by 1335. As many as 62 friars from several houses were admitted in 1318 by Bishop Dalderby to hear confessions within the diocese. Notable benefactors included Henry de Lacy, Earl of Lincoln, d1311, and bishops Thomas Bek in the 1340s and William Alnwick in the 1440s, and Ralph, Lord Cromwell in the 1450s. Provincial chapters of the Premonstratensians were held here in 1459, 1476 and 1489, and an earlier chapter had been held in the church of the Friars of the Sack (see text on page 66, and also picture on page 62).

In 1534 the friars were allowed to take stone from the nave of a nearby disused church for the repair of their buildings, and in 1535 a roof from another disused church was made available to them and they were allowed to lay a new water conduit. When the friary was surrendered to the Bishop of Dover in 1539 the mayor was keen to obtain the conduit for the use of the townsfolk. A free grammar school established in the precinct in 1568 was later handed over to the mayor and townsfolk.

The city museum now occupies the 30m long building of the 1240s now thought to have been the infirmary. Originally it was a single storey hall with eight paired lancets on the north, seven to the south and three lancets surmounted by a vesica in the east end wall. A blocked two bay arcade with an octagonal pier at the west end of the north wall opened into a chapel. In the late 13th century a vault was inserted, creating a lower room nine bays long with single-chamfered ribs springing from a central row of octagonal piers. A new chapel was then partitioned off at the east end of the upper level, where there is a piscina on the south and an east window with intersecting tracery. An original roof of that period survives with two collars with a semicircular arch below, whilst the west end, perhaps slightly later, has scissor braces. The rest of the buildings extended northwards with the church up near Silver Street. Excavations in 1994 found footings of the refectory range, a kitchen with huge hearths west of it, plus traces of the reredorter near a precinct gateway.

Vaulted undercroft at Lincoln Greyfriars

LINCOLN   Lincolnshire   *Friars of the Sack*   SK 975714   East of lower part of town

The Friars of the Sack were settled in Lincoln by 1266 when Henry III allowed them to take over a vacant plot next to their house in the suburb of Thornbridgegate Street. In 1268 he gave them thirteen oaks towards building their church. Lands given by other benefactors eventually gave them a precinct as large as 160m by 125m. After 1274 houses of this order were forbidden to take in new members, and although there were still four friars here in 1300, they seem to have gone by 1307. In that year the Premonstratensian abbey of Barlings tried unsuccessfully to obtain the site, which was to have been made into warehousing. The church was still usable in 1310 when a provincial chapter of Premonstratensian abbots was held within it, and arrangements were made in 1327 for the support of some chaplains to serve it, but the rest of the site was granted to Philip de Kyme in 1313. A chantry chapel of St Peter served by five priests was founded on the site in 1359 by Nicholas de Cantilupe's wife Joan, previously widow of Philip de Kyme's son William.

LITTLE WHELNETHAM   Suffolk   *Crutched Friars*   TM 887588   6km SE of Bury

The SE corner buttress is the only remaining part of the chapel of St Thomas of this friary founded in 1274. A small amount of flint walling survives of a medieval range extending southwards within the west range of a house of the early 16th century currently undergoing modernisation. Excavations have revealed more medieval wall footings of this range further north. The house has brick walls to the outside world but timber-framed walls towards a tiny court to the east of the former medieval range. In the east range the upper storey has four small windows in a room at the north end next to where the chapel lay which look as though they allow for friars' beds in a dormitory, which suggests that the house may at least partly pre-date the closure of the friary.

The house of the Crutched Friars at Little Whelnetham

LONDON   *Augustinians*   TQ 329815   Near to the Bank of England

The street called Austin Friars (actually a network of alleyways) recalls the Augustinian friary founded in 1253 set against the north side of the city wall. As rebuilt in the 14th century the church was 80m long and had an aisled nave with a clerestory. After the Suppression the nave remained in use for worship by Dutch Protestants. It was destroyed by bombing in 1940 and a church of 1950-7 now lies on the site.

LONDON   *Carmelites*   TQ 314813   Beyond Ludgate, west of St Paul's

A late 14th century vaulted crypt from the prior's lodging still remains of this friary, which extended from Fleet Street to the River Thames, and is commemorated by the name Whitefriars Street. The crypt was rediscovered in the 1920s when the News of The World offices were built in Boverie St, and later moved on a concrete raft to where it can be seen behind no 63 in Fleet Street. In 1385 Richard II issued a licence for the crenellation of a chamber block (probably guest accomodation) within the precinct. The friary went to the royal doctor William Butte after being suppressed, and in the late 16th century its hall was used as a theatre. The church was about 80m long and had an aisled nave with a clerestory.

LONDON   *Crutched Friars*   TQ 336809   To north of the Tower of London

The street name Crutched Friars near Fenchuch Street station commemorates this friary about which little is known. It existed from 1244 to the end of the 13th century.

LONDON   *Dominicans*   TQ 317811   To the west of St Paul's Cathedral

The Dominicans originally arrived in London in 1221 but moved from Holborn in 1276 to a new site between Ludgate Hill and the River Thames once occupied by a fortress called Montfitchet's Tower. Originally this site was acquired by the Dominicans as a quarry for building work on the Holborn site. Edward I was a generous benefactor and allowed the city wall to be re-aligned to fit around their precinct. Nothing survives above ground but the full layout of the buildings is known. Excavations in 1989-90 found the east end of the church, what was probably the east wall of the chapter house, the north wall of the nave and a possible base of an arcade pier (see page 11).

At about 66m long the church shorter than the London churches of the Augustinians, Carmelites and Franciscans. A cross-passage surmounted by a tower lay between a choir six bays long and a fully aisled nave of seven bays. Beyond the three western bays of the north aisle was a Lady chapel and on the south side of the choir was a long narrow sacristy. To the south was a large cloister with guest rooms in the west range and a kitchen in the corner between it and the refectory on the south side. The chapter house projected from the east range and the prior's lodging lay between it and the sacristy. The dormitory lay over the east range and the eastern cloister walk.

To the SE lay a smaller second cloister with the infirmary buildings arranged around it. To the south of the kitchen lay another room and then the chapel of St Anne, beyond which extended to the south a large hall used for parliaments and privy council meetings. Here in 1529 were staged Catherine of Aragon's divorce hearings. After suppression the site was granted to Lord Cobham. A theatre was built on part of the site in the late 16th century by James and Richard Burbage and the Society of Apothecaries held meetings in the friary precinct gatehouse from 1632 until it was destroyed in the great fire of 1666. The former King's Printing House of 1740 incorporated cellars from the friary and part of the cloister wall still remains on the north side of Ireland Yard.

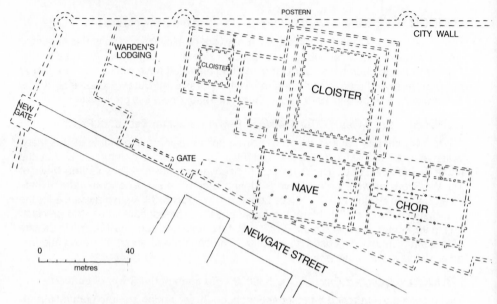

POSTERN

CITY WALL

WARDEN'S LODGING

CLOISTER

CLOISTER

NEW GATE

GATE

NAVE

CHOIR

0   40

metres

NEWGATE STREET

Plan of the former Franciscan friary in London at 1:1600 scale

LONDON   *Franciscans*   TQ 318814   To NW of St Paul's Cathedral

This friary founded in 1224 lay between Newgate Street and the city wall just east of the NW corner. Following a rebuilding of 1306 - 27 it had the largest friary church in the British Isles, in which were buried Edward I's second wife Margaret, Edward II's wife Isabella, and the heart of Henry III's wife Eleanor. The church was 91m long by 27m wide, being a fully aisled rectangle with a central passage between a nave and choir each of seven bays. It contained a row of four chapels at the east end of the nave, altars at the end of each of each of the aisles of the nave and choir, a high altar in the choir and a chantry chapel halfway along each of the choir aisles, making eleven altars in total. Sacristies flanked the eastern three bays of the north aisle of the choir. After the friary was closed in 1538 the church was used by Christ's Hospital, founded in 1552. Christchurch, a church of 1677-87 designed by Sir Christopher Wren, now lies on the site of the choir, whilst the Post Office now has buildings over the western part of the site, beyond where the nave once lay.

North of the nave was a cloister about 40m square. The east range contained the dormitory over the chapter house and study rooms. The west range contained the refectory and the north range contained a large library. The infirmary and various other rooms surrounded a smaller second cloister to the west.

LOSSENHAM   Kent   *Carmelites*   TQ 840278   18km north of Hastings

Sir Thomas Archer founded this friary in the parish of Newenden c1244. He was buried in the choir and his descendents remained patrons until the 16th century. The friary was burnt down by malefactors in 1275. Here lived friar William Stranfield, 1390, who wrote a history of the Carmelite Order. After the friary was surrendered to the Bishop of Dover in July 1538 he reported that there was no lead on the buildings, which were then ready to fall down and have now vanished without trace. A farm lies on the site.

LUDLOW   Shropshire *Augustinian*   SO 511743   South of the town centre

This friary was founded c1254, and Brian de Brampton was an important early benefactor. The friars were allowed to enclose an adjoining lane between Old Street and
Galford in 1284, and in 1326 they acquired two and half acres of meadow adjoining
their house. There seems to have been a dozen friars here in 1290. Bishop Swinfield
of Hereford denounced a violation of sanctuary here in 1299. Fragments of sedilia with
ball-flowers and tiles with the Beauchamp arms found on the site suggest the church
was completed in the mid 14th century. It was nearly 60m long and had a north aisle,
whilst the large cloister and buildings lay to the south. A provincial chapter was held
here in 1426. The community probably declined after the town was sacked by the Lan-
castrians in 1459. It appears that some of the furnishings were disposed of before the
last four friars surrendered in August 1538, but there were still some new choir stalls
and three bells in a steeple. This was unusually located at the NE corner of the choir
which survived until it was sold to the corporation for its materials in 1572. A gateway
and precinct wall survived until 1817. The site became a cattle market in 1860.

LUDLOW   Shropshire *Carmelites*   SO 511750   North of the town centre

In 1353 Sir Laurence de Ludlow was buried in the choir of the church of the friary at
the bottom of Corve Street that he had founded in 1350, when the prior and three friars
were licensed to hear confessions throughout the diocese of Hereford. In 1355 they
were pardoned for acquiring more land and demolishing buildings to make way for the
cloister buildings. Rents remained payable on some of the land. From the evidence of
wills it is clear that the church was still under construction in the 1380s, and it was enlarged in the 15th century, resulting in what John Leland called "a fair and costly thing"
with its choir "well stalled about". A provincial chapter was held here in 1416.

The friary was sacked along with the town by the Lan-
castrian army in 1459. Five friars surrendered it in August
1538, when there is a mention of furnishings for the infirmary, the buttery and kitchen, the prior's chamber, the
upper chamber, other chambers, the choir, a chapel containing a tomb of Robert Mascall and two sacristies. Most
of the buildings seem to have been demolished by 1558,
but the choir is said to remained in use as a chapel serving
some still surviving almshouses built nearby in the 1590s
by Charles Foxe of Bromfield. He brought over two bells
from his cellar to hang in the steeple. The chapel roof became dangerous and was taken off c1740 but the walls
stood until c1800. A carved head over a gateway is the
only visible relic of the medieval buildings.

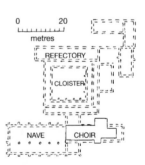

Plan of Ludlow Carmelite Friary

Lying on the site of the choir is the 19th century church
of St Leonard, now offices. West of it lay a tower over a
cross-passage and then a nave and south aisle with an
arcade of six bays, the latter a presumed 15th century addition. Rather unusually there seems to have been a range
between the church and the cloister to the north, beyond
which was the refectory. The chapter house projected
from the middle of the east range but there was no west
range. There was also a large L-shaped block to the NE.

Head at Ludlow Carmelite Friary

MALDON   Essex   *Carmelite*   TL 850069   On south side of the town centre

Richard Hely, Prior of Maldon wrote an account of the Carmelite houses of England in which he placed his own friary twenty-sixth in order of foundation out of forty. In 1293 Richard Gravesend, Bishop of London and Richard Iselham, Rector of South Hanningfield were allowed to grant the friars a five acre plot in Maldon. The friary lay close to the gaol in the parish of All Saints and initially there were difficulties with the canons of Beeleigh, who held the church. Under an agreement made in 1300 the friars were to pay 5s annually to the abbey, to only hear confessions when licensed to do so by the curate, and all burial fees would go to the parish church. In 1391 Pope Boniface IX granted relaxation of penance in return for gifts to the chapel of St Mary. The friary had an annual income of just £1 6s. 8d shortly before it was surrendered to the Bishop of Dover in 1538, making it one of the poorest monastic houses in England. At least part of the buildings were still occupied as a mansion by Vincent Harris in 1570. Excavations in 1991 to the rear of White House Lane revealed the north and east parts of a cloister 27m wide and part of a building to the north of it, probably the church.

MARLBOROUGH   Wiltshire   *Dominican*   Unknown location to south of town

Land for the foundation of this friary was given in 1315 by William de Rammeshulle and John Godhyne. Documents refer to the latrine block being used as a landmark and the rape of a child by one of the friars. After being surrendered to the Bishop of Dover in July 1538 the friary was said to have "no lead and only a little steeple".

MELCOME REGIS   Dorset   *Dominican*   SY 680790   In the centre of Weymouth

In 1418 Pope Martin V gave permission for Sir Hugh Deverell and John Rogers to found what was to be the last Dominican house in England. The founders then handed over two messuages, two tofts and four curtilages to Prior Edward Polyng and two other friars. Initial hostility from the Bishop of Salisbury was overcome by a petition claiming that Melcome was over a mile and a half from the parish church at Radipole and was Godless, lawless and open to the king's enemies. The friary lay in Maiden Street close to the shore, in what is now the middle of Weymouth, and in the 1440s the friars were the prime movers in the building of a new jetty which acted as a sea-defence.

16th century building, possibly a relic of Newark Friary

The inventory of furnishings taken after the house was surrendered in September 1538 includes new altars, new stalls and the tomb of Owen Watson, Rector of Portland, who was buried here in 1533, whilst there was a single bell in the steeple. There was little of value in the parlour, buttery, kitchen and vestry and the chambers contained only four old bedsteads, a feather bed and a flock bed. The buildings survived in ruins in 1650 and the church was still being used as a malt-house in 1803, but the remains were levelled in 1861 and the site divided into building plots.

MOTTENDON   Kent   *Trinitarian*   TQ 818464   At a farm 11km SE of Maidstone

The farmhouse beside a 13th century double system of moats incorporates a 16th century building partly of brick with stone arched windows which is all that remains of the Trinitarian friary founded shortly before 1236 by Robert de Rokeslay. In 1404 Richard de Berham managed to compel the minister of Mottendon to honour an agreement to supply two friars to celebrate mass in the chapel at Sissinghurst. In the Bodleian Libary at Oxford is a 15th century book of collected logic and grammar from the library of this friary. Here in 1499 was buried Peter Husey, Archdeacon of Northampton. After the Suppression the friary and its lands went to Henry VIII's minister Thomas Cromwell. Four of the friars were still receiving pensions in 1555. In the 1560s there were still people that could remember the annual procession and pageant on Trinity Sunday at the friary at Mottendon. In this show the chief feature was the friars' using holy water to repel an attack by a devil. Excavations have revealed traces of the south wall of the church and the adjoining north cloister alley along with 13th and 14th century pottery.

NEWARK-ON-TRENT   Nottinghamshire   *Observant Franciscans*   SK 801541

Henry VII introduced Observant Francicans here in c1499 and in 1509 left them the very considerable sum of £200 in his will. His son Henry VIII had all of the Observant Franciscan houses emptied in 1534 and at Newark some Augustinian friars used the premises until closure in 1539. The dispossessed Observants were treated very badly. Warden Gabriel Peacock became a prisoner in the Lincoln friary, whilst Hugh Payne died a prisoner in the Marshelsea prison in London after being arrested on the point of taking ship at Cardiff for the offence of collusion with the rejected former queen, Catherine of Aragon. The two altered buildings now remaining and in use as private dwellings on the east side of Appleton Gate in the NE corner of the town may date from after the 1530s. Neither can be identified as being part of the usual layout of a friary although such may never have existed here since the friars may have taken over existing buildings which may possibly have been previously used by Augustinian friars.

NEWCASTLE-UNDER-LYME   Staffordshire   *Dominicans*   SJ 846459

On SW side of town centre

This friary existed by 1277 when Edward I sent money for a day's food for twenty friars, although when Edward II visited the town in 1323 there were only twelve friars. Numbers must have increased again for in 1361 Henry, Duke of Lancaster aided the friars in gaining more property "for the enlargement of their house". In 1490 the Dominican minister general appointed William de Barleton as his vicar with power to gather into the Newcastle house "the devout brethren of the Observance", ie those friars which still adhered to the original strict standards of the order. In 1538 the Bishop of Dover found the house in a very poor state with the cloister roofs about to collapse, the church furnishings all old and decrepit and the community £20 in debt, whilst most of the buildings and lands had been leased to Henry Broke. The lead on the choir and cloister roofs plus other roofs of slate were the main items of any value. The bishop's inventory of the contents lists two feather beds in the dormitory, the refectory tables and trestles, a few utensils in the kitchen and bakehouse and three chests of documents, 'the one of the king's, the other of gentlemen's, the third of the convent's". A cattle market later stood on the site of the friary to the east of the castle where Blackfriars Road meets Goose Street. Nearby streets are called Friarswood Road and Friars Lane and the Lyme Brook is thought to have flowed through the precinct.

NEWCASTLE-UPON-TYNE   *Augustinian*   NZ 253642   On east side of the city

William, Lord Roos is thought to have founded this friary shortly before 1291, when John de Capella was licensed to provide it with more land, and by 1299 it appears to have had ten friars, whilst this had increased to twenty-four by 1322. In 1306 they were given another long strip of land to enlarge their cemetery, and other gifts of land followed in 1309, 1322 and 1331. Richard II issued a writ to cause the bailiffs of the town to prevent ditches and streets around the friary being littered with rubbish and sewage "to their great annoyance and peril". Henry VII's daughter Margaret stayed in the friary on her journey north in 1503 to marry James IV of Scotland.

After being surrendered early in 1539 by Prior Andrew Kel and his seven brethren and three novices the friary was retained by the crown for the use of the Council of the North as an occasional alternative to meetings at York. It was also then used as a munitions store and magazine and was described by John Leland c1540 as having "three or four faire towers belonging to it". The buildings were dismantled in the early 17th century and the town corporation built the Holy Jesus Hospital on the site beside City Road in 1681. To the rear of the east end of this brick building is the Tower of the Manors, a 16th century structure with its south side incorporating part of the north wall of the choir of the friary church, whilst the west wall includes part of the sacristy. An effigy of a knight found during an excavation here now lies within the tower.

NEWCASTLE-UPON-TYNE   *Carmelite*   NZ 248637   SW corner of the city

In 1307 the Carmelites took over the former premises of the Friars of the Sack between the West Gate and the River Tyne, their original site established in the 1250s at Wall Knoll having been cut down in size by the construction of the town defences. There were 25 friars at Wall Knoll in 1299 and in 1361 the original site was handed over for the founding of Holy Trinity Hospital. Prior Gerald Spor and seven brethren and two novices surrendered the friary early in 1539. A new house was built in 1740 on the site which adjoins Forth Street and Orchard Street.

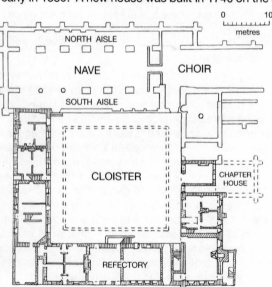

Newcastle Augustinian Friary   *Plan of Newcastle Dominican Friary at 1:800 scale*

Chapter House entrance at Newcastle Dominican Friary

NEWCASTLE-UPON-TYNE   *Dominican*   NZ 244642   On west side of city

The Dominicans arrived in Newcastle by 1239 and in 1250 the prior of the friary here was criticised for his architectural extravagance by the General Chapter of the Order. Sir Peter Scot and his son Nicholas are said to have been major benefactors c1260.The friars were allowed in 1264 to build a conduit to bring in a water supply and in 1280 to make a postern gate through the recently erected town wall which divided their property. The ditch outside the postern was spanned by a small removable timber bridge. In 1299 there were thirty-three friars here. In 1318 land which had belonged to the recently hanged Gilbert de Middleton was handed over to the friars and another slice of land was acquired by the friars in 1330 in order to enlarge the friary. In 1334 Edward Balliol did homage for the kingdom of Scotland to Edward III in the friary church here. In 1342 Edward III allowed the friars to re-erect gates on their land torn down during a dispute between the townsfolk and the men of the county of Northumberland. In 1397 a provincial chapter was held here, mainly to discuss certain apostate friars on whom Richard II had ordered a prohibition of the conferring of masters' degrees.

The house was surrendered by the prior and twelve friars in 1539 and in 1544 was granted to the mayor and burgesses of Newcastle. The church was then dismantled but its layout is known from excavations and is marked on the ground. The aisled nave had six bays with the end bays longer than the others. The piers stood on big oblong bases except for two at the west end on the south side. In 1552 the corporation leased the remaining buildings to nine of the town's craft companies, each of which took a third of one of the east, south or west ranges, and then altered their portion to provide a meeting room over an almshouse. The families living here in crowded and insanitary conditions were removed in the 1930s but the buildings (beside Monk Street) survived to be restored in the 1970s to provide craft shops, a restaurant and other rooms. The west range has survived in a more complete state than the others and has on the each side, facing the former cloister, a partially blocked up lavatorium recess. The south range has been mostly rebuilt, especially at the west end. The east range has lost its northern end and the projecting east end of the chapter house but a fairly complete lower room remains at the south end with three original lancets in the end wall.

NEWCASTLE-UPON-TYNE   *Franciscans*   NZ 252640   On east side of the city

The Franciscans were established in Newcastle probably as early as the 1230s with the Carlisle family of merchants as major benefactors. It was the head house of a wardenship which by 1258 included three other houses in England and five in the southern half of Scotland. There were thirty-three friars here in 1299 but only twenty-four in 1322. The celebrated scholar Dr John Scot, also known as Duns Scotus, who excelled at Oxford, began his education in this friary in the 1280s. It appears that he was a native of Northumberland, although both Ireland and Scotland have claimed to be his place of origin. He moved to Paris in 1304 and then was sent by the head of the order to Cologne in 1308 where he died that year of apoplexy, aged just thirty-four. In his wake came Hugh of Newcastle or the Scholastic Doctor, who died here in 1336.

The friary lay close to the Pilgrim Gate and was fed with water from a spring at the top of the Lork Burn, the supply being shared with the townsfolk, who, however abused the privilege, breaking the conduit and changing its course, so that in 1342 Edward III allowed the friars to wall in and lock up the water source. Henry VII expelled the Conventual Franciscans from this house and installed some Observant Franciscans instead. They opposed Henry VIII in 1534 and were in turn removed and replaced by Conventuals who lasted here just until January 1539 when the house was surrendered by Prior John Cragforth, eight friars and two novices.

NORTHALLERTON   N. Yorkshire   *Carmelites*   SE 371942   In middle of town

This friary was founded in 1356 by Edward III, John Yole, and Thomas Hatfield, Bishop of Durham, who donated six acres of land for it to be built upon. The friary church was the burial place of Marion, sister of John Neville of Raby, who had built it and left £100 in his will in 1386 towards further works. John's son Ralph, 1st Earl of Westmorland gave £40 towards the kitchen and other houses. Prior William Humfrey and five friars and five novices surrendered the house in December 1538.

NORTHAMPTON   Northants   *Augustinians*   SP 752602   SW of town centre

The earliest references to the Augustinian friary here date from 1275 to 1290. It was added to by Sir John Longville of Wolverton in 1323 and in 1330 George Longville was licensed to donate more land. In October 1538 the friary was surrendered to Dr London by Prior John Goodwyn and eight other friars. The prior was imprisoned for a time for disposing of the plate before the surrender, whilst the lead from the roofs was set aside for use on a possible new royal lodge at Grafton Regis.

NORTHAMPTON   *Carmelites*   SP 756605   In the middle of the town centre

This friary was founded in 1271 by Simon Montford and Thomas Chitwood. In 1278 an enquiry was held concerning an application by the friars to block off access to a section of the town wall and to block the crenels on its parapet, whilst in 1400 another enquiry investigated a claim that the friars had sheltered some robbers that had escaped from imprisonment in the castle. Bishop Dalders in 1310 allowed the friars to have five altars in their church, which like most Carmelite churches was dedicated to St Mary, and he issued an additional licence for the dedication of an altar to St Catherine. Prior John Howell and eight other friars surrendered the friary in October 1538 to Dr London, who reported that although the choir had a new roof of slates the sale of the contents of the friary, which were mostly old and of little value, would not cover the extent of the community's debts. Excavations have revealed minor remains.

NORTHAMPTON   *Dominicans*   SP 751606   To the west of the town centre

Hugh Wells, Bishop of Lincoln endorsed the establishment of the Dominicans in the centre of the town c1230. Henry III was a generous benefactor, donating oaks from royal forests on several occasions such as in 1249, when the friars' church was ready to be roofed. Dead trees in the royal forests were also sometimes donated for fuel. Already in 1239 there had been sufficient accommodation for a provincial chapter to be held here and there is a mention in 1259 of the erection of study-rooms. Edward I also contributed gifts of oaks, as in 1278 and 1286, when further work was done on the church, perhaps referring to its nave. In 1279 Queen Eleanor gave the friars a spring called the "Floxewell" from which water was brought into the friary by an underground conduit. Other provincial chapters were held here in 1271, 1272, 1284, in 1313 when Edward II donated £15 for three days food for the assembly, and in 1361. During the 15th century several provincial chapters of Premonstratensian canons were held in this friary, presumably because of its fairly central position.

Two small extra plots of land were acquired in 1301, but in 1358 crown officials took possession of some properties acquired for enlargement but actually let to tenants for annual rents. Edward III returned the properties on condition that their space was in fact used for enlarging the friars' house. There seem to have been thirty-six friars here in 1329 and thirty-three in 1335. One of the friars of this period was Robert Holcot, who took the degree of D.D. at both Oxford and Cambridge. Most of his works, which included twenty-six treatises on theology and philosophy, eventually found their way into printed books over a century after his death here from the plague in 1349 whilst ministering to sick townsfolk. In the British Museum is a charter recording the admission here by Prior Richard Metteley in 1511 of Robert Greenway and his wife Alice as lay members of the Dominican order. The standardised form of the document suggests that this was a common occurrence, although records of it rarely have survived. The Valor of 1535 records the friary as having an annual revenue of over £5 after annual payments due to the abbey of St James and to the mayor and bailiffs had been made, making it richer than the majority of friaries, although still poor compared with most other types of monastic houses.

NORTHAMPTON   *Franciscans*   SP 758608   To NE of town centre

There were Franciscans in Northampton soon after they first arrived in England in 1224. They lived in a house in the parish of St Giles outside the western walls of the town. In 1235 John of Reading, Abbot of Oseney resigned his office and joined the friars here. They later moved to another site on the NE side of the town which John Leland describes as "a little beyond the chief manor place". Edward I told the sheriff in the 1270s to take back a horse and cart which had been given as a royal gift but which had run down and killed a citizen. In 1278 the king provided four oaks from Silverstone Forest, and in 1291 he licensed the friars to construct a water conduit over several private properties between their spring and their house. In October 1538 the friary was surrendered by Warden John Wyndlowe and ten other friars to the king's commissioner Dr London, who reported that the church was covered with lead. Parts of the church and another range were found during excavations in the mid 1970s.

NORTHAMPTON   *Friars of the Sack*   Location Unknown

Little is known about this community except that it was founded during Henry III's reign by Sir Nicholas de Cogenoe and presumably died out by the early 14th century.

NORWICH   Norfolk   *Augustinian*   TG 234084   On SE side of city centre

Roger Mingot provided a messuage for creating a house of Augustinian friars here c1275. Edward I in 1293 allowed them to acquire and demolish five adjoining tenements to make space for their buildings. Further land was obtained in 1325 and 1335, and in 1348 the church of St Michael Conesford was taken within their precinct on condition that they maintained a chapel there and that three masses a week were said for the souls of the Thorp family. In 1457 Margaret Wetherby asked in her will to be buried beside her husband Thomas in the friary church and left 100 marks for building a new library on condition that the names of the couple were inscribed on the glass of the windows and on the book-rests. Members of the Bigod, Clifton, Hastings, Morley, Ufford and Wyndham families were also buried in the church, which was large and had a cloister on the south side. Within it were held services connected with the guilds of St Christopher, St Margaret, the Holy Cross and St Augustine connected with the shoe-makers. The Lady chapel of the church was privileged to also be known as a Scala Celi or Ladder to Heaven, to which special indulgences were granted, the only other ones in England being at Boston and Westminster. An early 14th century stone arch in Fleur de Llys House south of Morgan's Brewery in King Street may be a relic of the friary.

NORWICH   Norfolk   *Carmelite*   TG 235093   To north of city, beyond the river

A merchant called Philip founded this friary in 1256 beside his own house in Cowgate between the river and St James's Church, and he later joined the community, dying there in 1283. Further land was acquired by the friars from the rectors of Tivetshall and Beighton, and there were other gifts in 1332 and 1345, whilst Edward III allowed the enclosing of lanes adjoining the friary. A new church was dedicated in 1343 by John Paschal, Bishop of Llandaff, acting as suffragan for the Bishop of Norwich. Another dedication in 1382 by Thomas, Bishop of Sentari, another suffragan, probably marked the completion of the nave. In 1488 the mayor and corporations were formerly adopted as patrons of the friary and in 1498 granted it the privilege of exemption from all tolls. Shortly before the house was surrendered late in 1538 an imposter who was Ralph Salter's servant John Pratte attempted to take possession of the friary, but was unable to produce any royal commission when challenged by the prior. For this offence he was sentenced to have both ears nailed to the pillory and then have them cut off.

The north end of the east range of Norwich Dominican Friary

Norwich Dominican Friary Church

NORWICH   Norfolk   *Dominican*   TG 231088   City centre, north of the castle

Dominicans first arrived in Norwich in 1226 to found the third of their English houses which originally lay beside the former parish church of St John the Baptist over-the-water given them by Sir Thomas Gelham. In 1289 Edward I gave the forty friars here 40s for three days' food and in 1291 they were given 100s from the estate of the late Queen Eleanor. In 1307 Edward II became the second founder by allowing the friars to transfer to a site formerly used by the Friars of the Sack, who had died out, the original site being subject to flooding and rather small for the flourishing community. Pope Clevent V sanctioned the move and this was confirmed by John XXII in 1317. Further land was soon acquired for the construction of a church and buildings large enough for sixty friars, Edward III ratifying most of the gifts and purchases after an inquisition was held in 1345 concerning the Dominicans taking up so much property in the city centre. There were 53 friars here in 1326 when Edward II donated money for a day's food.

The friary was gradually rebuilt during the mid 15th century following a fire of 1413 which consumed much of the city and killed two of the Domincan friars. During this period the friars made use of their original house and chapel across the river, known as Black Hall, which had been retained. Guilds associated with the church were that of St William which existed by 1251, and the Holy Rood which is mentioned in 1527.

In 1534 Prior Edmund Harcock got into trouble after preaching a sermon in front of the mayor and aldermen that was regarded as provocative. He was arrested and brought before the council but survived in office for another year until he referred to Henry VIII as the "so-called chief head of the Church of England" and was dismissed. The friary was surrendered in November 1538 to the Bishop of Dover shortly after the Duke of Norfolk had written to Thomas Cromwell describing the pitiful state of the mendicant friars in Norwich as "the old and small charity in these days is insufficient to live on, and they have ben fain to sell their goods; they made made no waste, but are slandered and inquieted by light persons breaking their glass windows"

Now known as St Andrew's Hall, the huge church 80m long dating mostly from c1440-70 is the only English friary church to survive complete, lacking only the octagonal tower above the central walking space which collapsed in 1712. Older parts are the seven-light window at the east end and the south aisle windows, whilst the south porch and the whole west end date from a restoration of 1863. The nave has lofty arcades with piers of four shafts with concave curves between them, above which is an ashlar clerestory with two windows in each of the seven bays. The choir has side windows of five lights with embattled and stepped transoms and the north aisle has four-light windows. There are traces of a former anchorite's cell near the NE corner.

The 14th century cloister on the north has a different alignment and it appears that the vaulted crypt known as Becket's Chapel at its SE corner may be a relic of a church earlier than the present one that was aligned with the cloister. Each of the vaulted alleys of the cloister lies within the lower level of a range and has four bays of quadruple-chamfered brick arches facing the garth, which is freely accessible to the public at all times. Only footings remain of the northern alley but modern buildings further out help to preserve the sense of enclosure. The dormitory on the upper floor of the east range retains one original tie-beam in the roof and one west-facing window. The sides of these ranges facing away from the cloister have been much rebuilt, that of the west range being late 19th century brick-work. Not much remains of the chapter house which had an unusual T-shaped plan, with an extra bay projecting to the east of what was otherwise a room three bays from north to south by two bays from east to west.

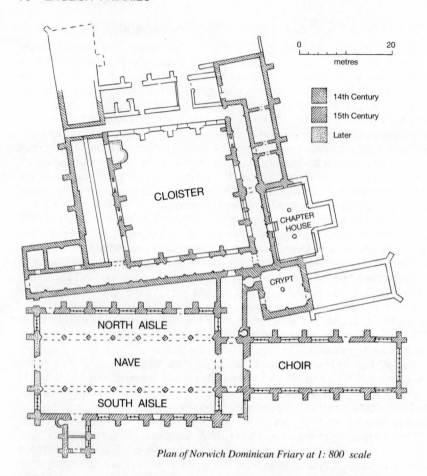

0   20
metres

14th Century

15th Century

Later

CLOISTER

CHAPTER HOUSE

CRYPT

NORTH AISLE

NAVE

CHOIR

SOUTH AISLE

Plan of Norwich Dominican Friary at 1: 800 scale

NORWICH   Norfolk   *Franciscan*   TG 235086   On east side of city centre

In 1226 the Franciscans established themselves on land in Conisford between the churches of St Cuthbert and St Vedast which was given by John de Hastingford. They were allowed to close off an adjacent lane in 1285 and in 1292 obtained further land from numerous benefactors, including the prior and convent of the cathedral-priory, the prior of St Faith's and the Abbot and convent of Holm. This enabled the layout of a large new church about 60m long with a cloister about 30m square on the north side of the nave. Three guilds, those of Our Lady, St John the Baptist and St Barbara, were connected with the church. The many bequests still on record include that of Roger Aylmer of 1492, who left money for "amending of their bokys and vestiments" and for "Fryer John Fisher of the said convent, be my prest, and to go to the court of Rome on pilgrimage, and say mass for my sowle at Seala Celi (Heaven's Ladder)." In March 1539 the site and buildings of the friaty were granted to the Duke of Norfolk, who had previously given the friars ("very poor wretches") 40s each to procure secular clothing. Traces of one building were revealed in an excavation near Prince of Wales Road in 1990. A bell-casting pit and part of the precinct wall were discovered in 1994.

NORWICH   Norfolk   *Other communities of friars*

The Dominicans later took over the premises formerly used by the Fiars of the Sack from 1258 until the early 14th century as already related. The Pied Friars are said to have had a house in the NE corner of the churchyard of St Peter Mountergate which was later used by the Master of the Hospital of Bek. In 1290 Roger de Tybenham left a lagacy to the Friars of St Mary or "De Domina". The lesser orders were supposed to be allowed to die out through lack of new recruits from 1274 onwards but these friars are said to have remained in residence on the south side of the churchyard of St Julian until they died of the plague in 1349 and their property passed into private hands.

NOTTINGHAM   Nottinghamshire   *Carmelites*   SK 571399   NW of town centre

Shortly before his death in 1272 Henry III granted ten oaks from a royal forest to the Carmelites for the repair of their church here. More land was given a few years later by Reginald, Lord Grey of Wilton along with numerous other small parcels of land from the townsfolk, the location being between Moothall Gate and St James's Lane in the parish of St Nicholas. In 1316 Edward II had contrived to have transferred to the friars the adjoining chapel of St James which had previously belonged to Lenton Priory. More land was obtained in 1319 and 1327, and in 1311 an association was set up to maintain the light of Our Lady in the friary church. Within the church Henry de Whitley took sanctuary in October 1393 after killing his wife Alice during the night.

In 1482 John Purvis was accused by Prior John Mott of leading an armed gang which broke into the friary and took goods valued at £23, including silver cups and two copes and there was a similar incident in 1495 when the draper Thomas Newton was accused of leading a gang that caused havoc in the friary grounds. The defendant had defaulted on a promise to repair the prior's house which had perhaps been damaged in an earlier raid. In 1496 another court hearing concerned the mason William Stark trying to recover money owing for the repair of the east window of the church. Yet another court action concerns a debt owed by Thomas Marsh, clerk of the vicar of Marnham to the friars for having celebated mass in the chapel of St James on the bridge over the River Trent for five weeks. Henry VIII visited the friary church in 1511 and in 1532 he issued a pardon to Prior Richard Sherwood for having struck friar William Bacon a mortal blow whilst they were drinking in a chamber of the house. Prior Roger Cappe and six other friars surrendered the friary in February 1539.

NOTTINGHAM   Nottinghamshire   *Franciscans*   SK 570394   To SW of town centre

The Franciscans settled in the SW corner of Broadmarsh near to the castle. In 1230 Henry III granted them twenty tie-beams for roofing their chapel. Further later gifts of wood were for stalls in 1232, a quay by the river in 1237 and for the infirmary in 1247. By 1256 rebuilding in stone had begun, and further oaks were later granted for work on the dormitory and chapter house. However the new church was not dedicated until 1303 and work on the aisles probably continued until the extra altars they contained were dedicated in 1310. Edward II allowed the friars to make an underground conduit through his park in 1311 to bring in water from a spring at Atherwell. Documents of 1359 and 1365 refer to an outside preaching cross near the precinct gateway. There are many records of small bequests to the friars in return for masses for the deceased. In 1522 the warden was in court on a charge of "baudre", and a previous warden had been implicated in a similar case back in 1500. Warden Thomas Basford and seven other friars surrendered the friary to the commissioner Dr London in February 1539.

ORFORD   Suffolk   *Augustinians*   Location Unknown

Augustinian friars here were given land by Robert de Howell in 1295, and they obtained more land in 1314, 1315 and 1337. Little else is known about the friary.

OXFORD   Oxfordshire   *Augustinians*   SP 516066   On north side of city centre

The Augustinians arrived in 1252 and in 1268 moved to a new site with Henry III and Sir John Handlow as the main benefactors. The latter was buried in the church and his descendants continued to maintain founders' rights and chambers in the precinct in the late 15th century. Others contributed extra land in 1269-70 and by 1289 there were enough buildings for a provincial chapter to be held here. Edward II gave the friars a quarry in Shotover Forest in 1316, and Edward III donated more land to allow for an establishment of fifteen friars plus students sent from other friaries and some servants. The huge church described by William of Worcester as having a nave and choir each sixty steps long once contained the early 16th century tomb of Walter Curzon and his wife now in the church at Waterperry. There were ten friars here when the house was suppressed in 1538. Wadham College built in 1610-13 now lies on the site.

The University soon established the custom that all those studying for B.A. degrees should dispute once and respond once within the Augustinian friary. Until the late 18th century all those aspiring to rise from a B.A. to an M.A. degree had to do "Austins", the custom surviving the closure of the friary. At one point in the 15th century the Augustinians were all suspended from the university for a verbal attack on their teachers but the Duke of Gloucester got them reinstated. In 1478 it was agreed that all friars had to feast the regent masters or pay a fee of ten marks to incept in divinity degrees.

OXFORD   Oxfordshire   *Carmelites*   SP 510065   On north side of city centre

In 1256 the Carmelites were given land near the hospital in Stockwell Street in the parish of St George. The friars soon ignored the agreement that they had made with Oseney Abbey not to take confessions. More land was obtained in the 1270s, and Henry III donated oaks for work on the church on four occasions, as did Edward I in 1276 and 1286. Chapters of the order were held here in 1264 and 1289. Nicholas de Catesby was outlawed for stealing books and other property from the friary but was pardoned in 1307. In Edward II's reign the friars transferred to a new site outside the north gate which had been a royal palace called Beaumont, however initially there were problems because this area had hitherto been much frequented by prostitutes.

In 1336 it was laid down that students staying here to study degrees had to have six referees and were not allowed to have servants. The Carmelites opposed John Wycliffe during his period of popularity in Oxford and after friar Peter Stokes made a reply to Wycliffe he walked the town in fear of his life. Henry IV gave the friary more land in 1401, whilst the pious and studious Henry VI who probably felt at home amongst the divines of Oxford is said to have used the friary as if it were his own palace. Later scandals here included a friar being imprisoned by the Proctor in 1501 for incontinence, a girl of thirteen being discovered in a student's cubicle in 1533, and a rivalry with the students of Gloucester College that led both parties being bound over to keep the peace. The buildings were said to be ruinous when surrendered in 1538 by Prior Richard Cheese and seven friars, plus two novices. Much of the stone from the buildings was taken off for work at St Frideswide's in 1546. The refectory remained in use as a poor-house to serve the parish of St Mary Magdalene until in 1596 it was demolished to provide materials for the building of a library at St John's College.

OXFORD   Oxfordshire   *Dominicans*   SP 512058   South end of the city centre

Within the first year of their arrival in England in 1221 the Dominicans settled in the Little Jewry area that was half in St Edward's parish and half in St Aldates parish and soon became embroiled in disputes with the canons of St Frideswide's. They seem to have initially run a house for Jews that were being converted to Christianity. Before long they began to build on a new location outside the town wall on lands given by Henry III, Isabel de Bolbec, and Walter Mauclerk, who in 1246 resigned the bishopric of Carlisle to join the Oxford friars. The king made frequent donations of timber and in 1258 gave £10 towards the building of a cloister. That year the so-called Mad Parliament in which the hostile barons presented Henry III with the list of demands known as the Provisions of Oxford met in the friary. In 1262 the church was consecrated by the Bishop of Lincoln, who had a lodging within the friary precinct.

In 1246 the general chapter of the order made provision for two friars from each house to be able to study at a "studium generale" or university and at another general chapter in Barcelona in 1256 it was ordained that English friars would study at Oxford, which was itself the venue for a general chapter in 1280 when there may have been as many as eighty friars in residence. About that time Edward I allowed the construction of a new water conduit into the friary. Here in 1314 lay the body of Edward II's favourite Piers Gaveston after he was executed by the jealous barons. A degree in those days was simply a licence to teach and under new University rules of 1310 no friar was allowed to lecture on the Bible until he had obtained a B.A. degree. The Dominicans protested that they had friars fit to lecture on the Bible but not qualified to lecture on the Sentences of Peter Lombard. The Archbishop of Canterbury supported the University's position but the friars appealed to the king, who wrote on their behalf to the Pope. In 1317 Pope John XXIII decided in favour of the friars, declaring that mendicant friars should not have to take preliminary degrees in arts, but the parliament held late in 1318 swung the royal power over to supporting the position of the University.

In 1330 the provincial prior was banished for supporting the rebellion of the Earl of Kent but he was reinstated later that year after Roger Mortimer, Earl of March fell from power and Edward III began to rule in his own name. The king later allowed the friars to have more land on which to build defences from flooding by the River Thames. In 1370 certain actions of the Dominican provincial prior caused the students here to rebel. In 1373 the king ruled that there were too many foreign students at Oxford, the implication being that some of them were acting as spies. Amongst the Dominicans it led to a rift between the English provincial and the General Chapter. There was a similar problem in the 1420s when the government considered that there were too many Irish friars studying at Oxford. There appears to have been a moral decline in the early 16th century, when the provincial prior in residence here was said to have sons and a mistress. When surrendered to Dr London in July 1538 the friary was said to have a large house covered in slates and a new church with a new choir covered in lead. The ten friars and an anchorite were all said to be willing to become secular priests.

The church may have still stood in ruins until the end of the 16th century. Excavations in 1979-80 revealed parts of the nave and its north aisle with later buttressing. Parts of the second of two cloisters were also found, along with a reredorter that was dismantled in the 14th century, the drain being robbed of all stone and backfilled. Of standing remains there are jambs of the precinct gateway in a cottage at the NW corner of the former chapel at the south end of Littlegate Street. On one side of it is a smaller pedestrian gateway.

OXFORD   Oxfordshire   *Franciscans*   SP 511059   SW end of the city centre

When the first two Franciscans arrived in Oxford in September 1224 they were given a warm welcome by the Dominicans and shared their dormitory and refectory for eight days until they were able to hire their own premises. Only later did the two orders fall out over the issue of the Franciscans' insistence on absolute poverty, which did however tend to give them the moral upper hand. Gradually the Franciscans were given bits of land in the parish of St Ebbe to create a precinct on the south side of what is now Church Street. The original buildings were modest and the infirmary was said to be barely high enough for a man to stand up in. In the chapel in 1235 was buried Agnellus of Pisa, who had led the first party of nine Franciscans into England in 1224. In 1238 a provincial chapter subsidised by Henry III was held here to protest against the tyranny of Elias, General Minister of the order. Other provincial chapters were held here in 1289, 1301 and 1405. The life these friars lived was harsh indeed, no pillows being allowed, nor any footwear except for the old and infirm. In 1233 they were joined by two canons who had escaped from Dunstable priory and c1240 both John, former abbot of Oseney and Ralph, former bishop of Hereford joined the friars.

The friars acquired more land, some of it outside the city wall, which was breached by a new postern in 1248 to allow access, an original plan to rebuild the city wall around the enlarged precinct having been abandoned. The north aisle of the new stone church of that period seems to have adjoined the city wall (remains of which have been found under the site now occupied by Sainsburys) resulting in a narrowing of the aisle towards the east end. In 1480 chapels were added on this side, resulting in several arches through the city wall. In all the church seems to have been about 75m long and contained several fine tombs, including that of Henry III's brother Richard, Earl of Cornwall and King of the Romans, who was a major benefactor. Edward III in 1346 granted the friars part of his quarry near Wheatley to provide stone for the repair of the friary. Minor fragments remain in Littlegate Street, and where Wood St meets Charles St.

The school founded by Agnellus was the largest of the early buildings. Early on he discovered the friars debating Utrum sit Deus? and exclaimed that "simple brothers enter heaven and learned brothers dispute whether there is a God at all!". Robert Grosteste became their first theological lecturer until in 1235 he was made Bishop of Lincoln. His three immediate successors also became bishops. Not until 1247 were the Oxford Franciscans friars taught by one of their own, Adam Marsh, although by this time other English friars had already taught in other houses and abroad. Adam Marsh had been an M.A. before he became a Franciscan friar and afterwards there was an ongoing dispute with the university, which was reluctant to allow friars to become doctors of theology without taking a degree in arts first, but this was forbidden by the constitutions of both the Franciscans and Dominicans. In 1358 the university forbade lay students to enter any of the mendicant orders until they were eighteen years old.

Latterly students were supposed to do eight years study of arts in their own houses and begin their nine year theology degrees there before moving to Oxford for higher instruction. They were then allowed to lecture on the Sentences which meant taking the degree of B.D. Another three years including the preaching of sermons were required for the degree of D.D. or S.T.P. but in practice friars sometimes managed to slightly shorten these lengths of time before degrees were awarded. Pope Benedict in 1338 tried to cut down the heavy expenses of inception which originally included feasting the masters. In Wycliffe's time a friar coming up from London to take a D.D. at Oxford was robbed of £40 although in 1478 the composition of a friar was fixed at 10 marks.

The stringency of the Franciscan rule had to be amended to accommodate lecturers, the other normal duties of friars being subordinated to their research and teaching. They were each allocated a separate chamber and had a socius or younger friar to act as their secretary and servant. They were supported by the convent where they taught but books and other expenses were provided by the convent, custody or province from which they had originally been sent. Students were supported by the convent that sent them unless they were lucky enough to have found a private sponsor, their annual livng costs of £5 per year being known as an exhibition. Iin 1292 the general chapter ordained that the number of foreign students should be equally divided between Oxford, London and Cambridge so as to ease the burden formerly put upon Oxford.

In 1454 William, Lord Lovell left the Oxford Franciscans the huge sum of 200 marks and there are records of many other bequests and gifts of that era. During that time there were separate libraries for the convent and the student friars. Bishop Grosteste had left the friars many valuable early books. In the 1530s one friar was accused of incontinence and another was seen "in a chamber at the sign of the Bear with a woman in a red cap". Eighteen friars surrendered the house to Dr London in July 1538.

OXFORD   Oxfordshire   *Crutched Friars*   Uncertain location to the east of the city

A new friary of the Holy Cross was founded in Oxford in 1342 to take thirteen friars send up from the London house to study in Oxford. In 1349 this community moved to a property near the East Gate owned by the Warden and fellows of Merton College. Foundations were laid of a chapel 15m by 9m but the Bishop of Lincoln stopped the work, either because of local clerical opposition or plague having killed the friars.

OXFORD   Oxfordshire   *Friars of the Sack*   Uncertain location to SW of the city

Friars of the Sack were given land in the parish of St Budoc c1262. Initially their chapel was only to be used by secular servants and sick inmates. Henry III gave them the ruined chapel of St Budoc in 1265 on the condition that the cemetery remained consecrated ground. Students were expected to read, write, pray, sleep and study in their own cells and were only expected to attend the daily chapter meetings on Wednesdays and Fridays. Each student was to have a copy of the Bible, the Sentences and the Histories. In 1296 the Pope ordered that the Franciscans were to be allowed to take over their premises after the last five Friars of the Sack here died out.

OXFORD   Oxfordshire   *Trinitarians*   Uncertain location to east of the city centre

The Trinitarians had students at Oxford by 1286 and with patronage from the Earl of Cornwall they established a friary in 1293 on land extending between the East Gate and St Friday Gate. In c1305 they acquired an adjacent chapel which was later served by friars from Hounslow, sold to the townsfolk in 1447, but recovered by the Trinitarians in 1486. The house at some point appears to have been moved to a new site within the city walls but was later decimated by the plague. In later years it was called Trinity Hall and had just a master and a few students, hardly any of whom were friars.

PENRITH   Cumbria   Augustinians   NY 518301   To the east of the town centre

The house called The Friars and the street called Friars Gate recall the former friary founded before 1300. John de Penrith donated more land to the friars in 1318, and John de Crombewell added some more in the 1330s. The prior was asked to send a friar to take services at Newton Reigny in 1360.

PLYMOUTH   Devon   *Carmelites*   SX 486546   To the east of the city centre

In 1288 John de Valletort gave a messuage and orchard to a few Carmelites from Bristol. By 1297 there were eight of them. They fell foul of the jealousy of the monks of Plympton and were placed under an interdict by Bishop Stapleton for preaching and taking confessions without licence, but Edward II eventually got this lifted. The friars were given some more land in 1329 and were left a bequest of 40s by Bishop Grandisson. However there were further quarrels over the friars' hearing confessions until 1375 when Bishop Brantyngham finally allowed them to do so. In September 1538 Prior John Mellyn and five friars surrendered the friary to the Bishop of Dover. In the 19th century a house called The Friary lay here until removed for a new railway station.

The 16th century stone-faced cob wall of the friary precinct extending south of Whitefriars Lane (now called Beaumont Road) towards Higher Street was greatly thickened internally after the Suppression to make a defensive enclosure which had a slight re-entrant angle on the east side, within which was a pond fed by a spring. Part of the gatehouse on the west side has been traced. Just east of it lay the church, which was aisle-less and about 55m long. It had a cloister 24m square on the south side with three ranges of buildings, with projections on the south and on the east, the latter being part of the chapter house. Excavations have revealed the southern end of the east range with a diagonal SE corner buttress and another buttress further west.

PLYMOUTH   Devon   *Dominicans*   SX 481541   At the east end of the town

A distillery now lies on the site of this friary which appears to have been founded as late as the early 15th century. After the three Plymouth friaries were surrendered in 1538 to the Bishop of Dover the site of this one went to the corporation of Plymouth.

The west end of the church of the Franciscan friary at Reading

PLYMOUTH   Devon   *Franciscans*   SX 481541   At east end of town centre

In c1384 Richard II allowed William Cole, Thomas Fisher, Geoffrey Couche and Humphrey Passour to provide six acres of land near Sutton Pool in the centre of the town for a new Franciscan friary. Bishop Brantyngham of Exeter took objection to the buildings being consecrated by John Bernham, supposedly as Bishop of Naples, and placed the community under an interdict. The prior was imprisoned for resisting the changes of the 1530s. After suppression in 1538 the site went to the Ilsham brothers and part of it was used as the Old Mitre Inn. Parts of the cloister with twisted spiral pillars survived as part of the inn courtyard until removed in 1813 to make way for the Exchange.

PONTEFRACT   West Yorkshire   *Dominicans*   SE 456217   SW end of town centre

When Edmund Lacy, son of the Earl of Lincoln died in 1257 he asked for his heart to be buried in the church of the friary that he had founded here the previous year, having donated an estate of about six acres called East Crofts, which he had obtained from the townsfolk. The stone he laid to begin the church supposedly immediately split in three in honour of the triple dedication to St Mary, St Dominic, and also St Richard, the latter a recent bishop of Chichester who had been a friend of Edmund and was not formerly canonised until a few years later. Another three and a half acres were given to the friars in 1309 by Walter de Baggehill, despite an unfavourable report from an inquisition over this. Slight traces of the friary buildings were found by excavation in 1988.

In 1267 several priors of Dominican friaries in northern England gathered here to arbitrate in a dispute between the Cluniac monks of the priories of Pontefract and Monk Bretton. In 1291 the friars preached in favour of a new crusade in Pontefract, Rotherham and Wakefield and they benefited from a 100s bequest from the estate of Queen Eleanor. In 1300 Edward I brought his second wife to stay at the friary on a couple of occasions, giving alms for food for twenty-nine friars as well as other gifts. It appears that there were as many as forty friars in 1310, when Edward II was at Pontefract. Other gifts of food when Edward III was staying in the town in the 1330s were for lesser numbers. Provincial chapters with royal sponsorship were held here in 1303 and 1321. One of the friars attended Thomas, Earl of Lancaster at his execution in 1322 after being defeated and captured at the battle of Boroughbridge. Lord Warine de Lisle, who was also then executed, was amongst the list of many nobles buried in the church, which also included members of the de Clare, Leybourne, and Vipont families, and also the hearts of Richard, Duke of York and his son Edmund and the bodies of others also killed during or after the battle of Wakefield. Prior Robert Dae and six other friars plus one novice surrendered the friary to Sir George Lawson and Richard Ballasis in November 1538. At least some of the buildings are recorded as having lead roofs.

PRESTON   Lancashire   *Franciscan*   SD 534294

The site of this friary was donated by the Preston family but Edmund, Earl of Lancaster from 1267 onwards was usually regarded as the founder and presumably paid for the construction of a large part of the buildings. His father Henry III had given the friars some oaks from a royal forest back in October 1260. The Archbishop of York asked the friars to preach in favour of a crusade in 1291. The friary was retained within the Worcester "custodia" as a result of a petition of 1330 by Henry, Earl of Lancaster when an administrative change was proposed, This friary seems to have survived until the early part of 1539, after which the site was sold to Thomas Holcroft for £126. It was later occupied by a foundry and then became railway sidings.

READING   Berkshire   *Franciscans*   SU 712736   North of town centre

The Franciscans arrived in Reading in 1233 and moved to the present site NW of the market place in 1285, their original location having proved damp and prone to flooding. Aided by a donation of 56 oaks from Edward I's royal forests work on the church was completed in the early 14th century. Of it there remain the aisled nave, which Henry VIII gave to the townsfolk for use as a guildhall, whilst other parts seem to have been used as a hospital, a poorhouse, and in the 18th century as a jail. There may have been some opposition to the surrender of the friary in September 1538 since the former warden and another friar from this community were recorded amongst the prisoners in the Tower of London in 1539. The transepts are of 1863, when the east bellcote was added and most of the external details of the rest were renewed. The arcades have moulded arches set on square piers with semicircular shafts. The large west window has reticulated tracery. The extension below it is of the 1970s. See photo on page 84.

RICHMOND   North Yorkshire   *Franciscan*   NZ 170010   North side of town centre

This friary just outside the northern walls of the town is thought to have been founded in 1258 by Ralph Fit-Randal of Middleham, whose heart was buried in the choir in 1270. Archbishop Romanus asked the friars in 1291 to preach in Richmond and in the deanery of Copeland in favour of a new crusade, and in 1315 the friars were asked to encourage local resistance to Scottish raids. In 1304 John of Brittany, Earl of Richmond left a bequest of £5 to the friars, and in the same year an apostate friar ran off with goods stored in the friary but was arrested and returned for punishment.

More lands were given to the friars in 1364 and 1383, and Sir Stephen le Scrope left them a generous bequest in 1406. Richard III ordered the receiver of Middleham in 1484 to pay the friars twelve and a half marks for the saying of a thousand masses for his late brother Edward IV. In 1490 it was decided that the friars should have the left over possessions of Margaret Richmond, who had been a Franciscan nun living as an anchoress in a small cell attached to the parish church, but that future anchorites would be chosen by the bailiff and twenty-four burgesses of the town. In January 1539 the friary was surrendered by Warden Robert Sanderson, thirteen other friars and a novice, all of whom were given small sums of money.

Still standing in a public park is quite an impressive tower with double-stepped battlements and eight short pinnacles which was later set into an early 14th century church of which parts of the choir north wall and the east wall of a south chapel or transept still remain with the outlines of windows. The tower is generally assumed to be 15th century although the responds of the arches on which it stands are still in a 14th century style. In 1998 parts of wide north and east ranges of the cloister buildings were found to be standing up to 2m high to the north of the tower but are not currently visible. Other remains were found to the NW. A medical centre now lies on the site of the cloister NW corner.

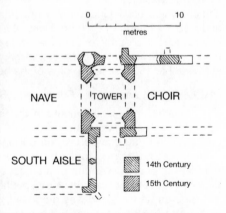

0 — 10
metres

NAVE   TOWER   CHOIR

SOUTH AISLE

14th Century

15th Century

Plan of the central part of the church of the Franciscan friary at Richmond

RICHMOND   Surrey   *Observant Franciscan*

SU 178748   To the SW of the parish church

This friary was one of six that were founded or refounded during the 1490s for Observant Franciscans by Henry VII. His son Henry VIII was also a generous benefactor and wrote to the Pope full of enthusiasm for the Observant Franciscans. It was only when they opposed his divorce in 1533 that he turned against them. Not all of them did oppose him and several private letters survive from Friar Laurence of the Richmond house to the king and his chief minister Thomas Cromwell. Hugh Rich, Warden of Richmond was amongst those accused of conspiring with Elizabeth Barton, "the Holy Maid of Kent", being executed at Tyburn in May 1534 after several months of imprisonment in the Tower of London. In the following months all efforts by Rowland Lee, Bishop of Coventry and Lichfield to get the friars at Greenwich and Richmond to acknowledge the royal supremacy failed and by the end of August the Observant Franciscans were suppressed in England and the friars were re-distributed amongst other Franciscan friaries. A few were allowed to go abroad but the majority were kept in chains and given hardly any food so that over fifty of them died within a year. The friary lay in Friars Lane close to the royal palace in which Edward III died in 1377 and Queen Elizabeth died in 1603. A house of c1700 called Old Friars is said to contain 16th century cellars. In 1649 there is a mention of the friary having had three rooms below stairs and four above, which suggests it never had a full set of cloister buildings.

The tower of the Franciscan friary at Richmond in North Yorkshire

RYE   Sussex   *Augustinians*   TQ 922204   At NE end of the centre of the town

The first mention of the friars here appears to be in 1368 when it was agreed that one of them should celebrate mass daily at the altar of St Nicholas in the parish church for William Taylour and his wife. Parts of the friary were re-roofed in 1524 at the expense of William Marshe. A much-altered chapel with windows with flowing tracery remains east of Conduit Street. It appears the friars transferred to this site in 1378. See p13.

RYE   Sussex   *Friars of the Sack*   TQ 921203   In the middle of the town

No 40 Church Square has a late 13th century window of two foiled lancets under a quatrefoil which is all that remains of the house of the Friars of the Sack established here c1263. The roof is also medieval but must date from after the friars had died out in the early 14th century. See picture on page 88.

SALISBURY   Wiltshire   *Dominican*   West of the town

In 1281 Edward I provided the Dominicans with land and hedging materials for founding a house in the western suburbs of the town, beyond the River Avon and opposite the site of the later gaol and infirmary. This community had originally occupied a site in West Street in Wilton, being granted oaks for building work by Henry III in 1245 and 1250. A cell may have continued to be used by Dominicans on the original site in Wilton in later years. In 1318 the friars were pardoned for their rescue of a prisoner condemned to death. The friary buildings were in good order when surrendered in the summer of 1538 to the Bishop of Dover.

House of Friars of the Sack, Rye

SALISBURY   Wiltshire   *Franciscan*   ST 147296   To the east of the cathedral

This friary is said to have been founded in the 1220s by Bishop Richard Poor, although there is doubt as to whether the Franciscans actually settled here before he was transferred to the see of Durham in 1228. Henry III in 1252 provided timber for enclosing the precinct. A provincial chapter was held here in 1510. When the friary was suppressed in 1538 Charles Bockley was already in residence and he offered £100 to purchase the buildings. A street called The Friary marks the site of the friary.

SANDWICH   Kent   *Carmelite*   TR 330580   On SW side of the town

The friary was founded in 1272 when Alderman Henry Cowfield donated some land. More land was given in 1280 by John of Sandwich and in 1292 by William, Lord Clinton, and an additional two acres was obtained by the friars in 1336. They were given a spring in Woodnesborough in 1300 along with leave to make an underground culvert. Prior Thomas Tulyet was one of those who testified against the Templars in 1311. Two of the friars were arrested in 1344 as having papal bulls and other papers prejudicial to the king's interests. In 1370 the Bishop of Exeter granted an indulgence of forty days to anyone visiting the image of St Catherine in the friary church. Those who left the friary large bequests included Sir Richard Atte Lease in 1393. The friary was surrendered to the Bishop of Dover in December 1538.

SCARBOROUGH   North Yorkshire   *Carmelite*   TA 045888   East of town centre

In October 1319 Edward II granted two houses to the Carmelites, having come to an agreement with the Cistercians in whose parish the property lay, and in March 1321 the Archbishop of York licensed the friars to build a chapel and bell-tower. A dispute over ownership of the land was only settled in 1341. The friars obtained more land c1325, and 1330, and an extra messuage in each of 1350 and 1358. Sir Robert de Roucliff also donated more land in 1362 and was later buried in the friary church.

In 1369 Prior Mauger de Baildon sued several people for debt and also took three chaplains to court for a serious assault upon Friar John Eryll. In 1370 the prior also sued the carpenter John Motsam to keep an agreement for the construction in the friary of a hall, chamber, study, cellar and a chapel, complete with doors and windows, two hearths and two sinks. In December 1537 Prior John Boroby was examined at York for collecting and distributing seditious prophecies and thus encouraging the rebels of the previous year. However he managed to remain in office until the friary was surrendered to the Bishop of Dover in March 1539.

SCARBOROUGH   North Yorkshire   *Dominican*   TA 044888   Middle of town

The Dominicans are first recorded in the town in 1252. They too had problems with the Cistercians who in 1285 claimed that the revenues they drew through the parish church had dropped to a third as a result of the Dominicans and Franciscans being in the town. The friary was one of 33 Dominican houses who were given 100s each from the estate of Queen Eleanor of Castile in 1291. A kinswoman of the late Queen named Isabel de Beaumont was married to the castle governor John de Vesci and she paid for the building of the nave of the church plus the cloister and dormitory. In 1291 the friars were asked by Archbishop Romanus to preach in favour of a new crusade in Pickering and Scarborough, and in 1293 he limited the friars claims to hear confessions.

In 1312 the unpopular favourite Piers Gaveston was persuaded to come out of the castle, where he was being besieged, and confer with Henry Percy and the earls of Pembroke and Surrey in the Dominican friary church. However once outside he was cut down and killed by the Earl of Warwick. In the years following this the friars were given several extra plots of land and ended up with about three acres. Two Scottish friars were washed up here from a shipwreck in 1327 but were carefully watched over by the town bailiffs as potential spies. Sir Thomas Ughtred left a bequest in 1398 for the augmentation of two chantries in the friary church founded by his ancestors. There were fifteen friars here in the 1490s. Prior John Newton and several other friars surrendered the friary to the Bishop of Dover in March 1539.

SCARBOROUGH   North Yorkshire   *Franciscan*   TA 046888   East of town centre

The Franciscans were settled here as early as February 1240 when Henry III ordered the sheriff of Yorkshire to provide food for them one day a week. The Cistercians soon took objection to their presence and in 1245 the king had the friars re-settled in a new location outside the town where a site of an acre and a half was available in the parish of Scalby. However in 1270 the friars moved back into the town onto a site given by Reginald the Miller, who was buried in the middle of the choir of the friary church. Sir Robert Ughtred later gave the friars extra land extending to the town wall which included a "gutter". In the 1280s the quarrel with the Cistercians broke out again, several abbots and bishops being involved in the case, which was eventually resolved in favour of the friars except that there may have been restrictions on them hearing confessions. In 1290 Pope Nicholas IV granted an indulgence to penitants visiting the friary church on the feasts of the Virgin, St Francis, St Anthony and St Clare. In 1291 Archbishop Romanus asked the friars to preach in favour of a new crusade in the towns of Bridlington and Whitby.

In 1290 Robert of Scarborough, Dean of Yarm left a bequest of 100 marks for providing a new water supply. The executor called in a debt from Meaux Abbey, who paid it in the form of sheets of lead taken off the roof of the dormitory of their lay brethren which were subsequently used to cover the church of the Franciscan friary at Scarborough. Forty fother of lead is mentioned by the Bishop of Dover, to whom the friary was surrendered in March 1539. The friars here also owned several cottages and a tavern.

All three friaries in Scarborough used to send an officer around the town with a handbell on the days of funeral obsequies of those buried in their churches and on the anniversaries of their founders and main benefactors. A royal licence for this obtained from Richard II in 1388 was withdrawn in 1389 after a protest by the Cistercians holding the parish church of St Mary as being an infringement of their rights, although the custom appears to have continued since it is mentioned in 1522.

SHOREHAM   Sussex   *Carmelite*   Original location probably now under the sea

Sir John de Mowbray founded this friary in 1316 and his father-in-law William de Bra-ose then gave an additional messuage. Land given in 1348 by Sir John de Mowbray allowed an extension northwards towards the High Street, whilst in 1326 the friars had obtained a house and chapel that had belonged to the Templars, and in 1368 they were left a bequest of £20 towards their church by Sir Michael de Poynings. By the late 15th century the site was under threat from the sea so the friars left and took a lease on an empty priory at Sele which had been suppressed and given to Magdalen College at Oxford. A house now stands on the site of it, beside Sele parish church, which is a composite building of various periods. In July 1538 it was discovered by the royal commissioner that the friars had all gone and the buildings left deserted and open.

SHREWSBURY   Shropshire   *Augustinian*   SJ 486127   SW of the Welsh Bridge

This house was founded c1254 for "the poor brethren of Coulon" a group of Tuscan hermits made welcome by Henry III and and established originally just north of the castle, although they soon moved to a location just outside walls near the Welsh Bridge. There appear to have been twenty friars by 1283. The Bishop of Lichfield in 1292 granted an indulgence to all those contributing towards building works. The church was completed in 1300 and they were then able to lease out the chamber that they had previously used for services. In 1337 the friars obtained from the borough a grant of a wall running down to the river called the 'new work" on condition that they built a substantial embattled house beside it and allowed the townsfolk to garrison it in the event of an attack. They were also allowed to create a postern gate through the wall to Rumboldsham. Provincial chapters were held here in 1383, 1389 and 1400. Here lived John Shipton, one of the twelve doctors who condemned Wycliffe in 1381. During this period Richard, Earl of Arundel was a generous benefactor.

By 1456 there were only six friars. A friar killed a man in self-defence in 1472 and took sanctuary in the church. Another man was killed in the affray which resulted when angry citizens attempted to pull him out of the church, and it was necessary for the king to intervene. A reconciliation with the townsfolk was affected by the Bishop of Carlisle and the Abbot of Shrewsbury. There are records of the friars being involved in no less that thirteen incidents of affray in the early 16th century, several of the cases being tavern brawls possibly resulting from Prior Richard Lyneal's rather short temper. Plague in 1525 caused the friars distress in that the supply of alms on which they depended almost dried up, although the borough made them some small grants.

In 1530 Prior William Man came to blows with the former prior John Towne and was bound over to keep the peace. In 1536 Prior Richard Alate was sent to prison after the burgesses discovered that stone from the friary buildings was being carted off. John Towne was then made prior again but the debts of the community continued to mount up since it had virtually no income. In August 1538 the royal commissioners found the buildings ruinous and empty of bedding, food or drink. The prior, said "like to be in frenzy" was dismissed and the only two other friars, who were both Irish, were ordered back to their native country, although they actually stayed on and in September 1539 were granted capacities along with two other friars.

Part of a ruinous red sandstone building with two doorways still remained in the early 19th century. It may have been the refectory block since the upper storey had a range of fine windows. Another doorway was discovered during alterations. Foundations of buildings were uncovered during construction of the Priory School on the site.

SHREWSBURY   Shropshire   *Dominican*   SJ 494127   To the south of the castle

The Dominicans were established on this riverside site close to the castle as early as 1232, when Henry III granted them 30 oaks and stone to build a church. Walter de Lacy's granddaughter and heiress Maud was a major benefactor c1250, as were her descendants from her subsequent marriage to Geoffrey de Geneville. In 1241-2 the friars were allowed to join their precinct wall to that of the town and benefited from two hundred cart loads of stone left over from the rebuilding of the town wall. In 1258 they were allowed to block off a lane which turned into a culvert and caused flooding when there was heavy rain. The precinct seems to have been extended into the river itself, which caused friction with the monks of the abbey, but the dean and canons of St Mary's looked upon the friars more kindly and donated a garden to add to their lands.

Provincial chapters of the order were held here in 1299 and 1345. In 1365 the friars were allowed to acquire land on the other side of the river which contained a well which they used as a water supply. In 1380 they were allowed to make a postern in the town wall to connect their precinct with lands they had acquired within the town wall. Prince Henry stayed in the friary before the nearby victory over the rebellious Percy family in 1403, where he was severely wounded in the face by an arrow. In 1431 the friars were accused of keeping ferrets and setting snares for rabbits with the town liberties as well as having enclosed some common land by St Mary's church. Here the Earl of March spent Christmas 1460 before taking the throne as Edward IV in January. In 1473 he sent his consort Elizabeth to the friary guest-house for the birth of their second son.

The Dominicans in Shrewsbury were better off than the other two orders of friars and consequently survived a visit in August 1538 by the Bishop of Dover, who wrote to Thomas Cromwell saying that he had no commission to suppress any house, his warrant being to take possession of those surrendered on account of poverty. However the friary was being demolished by October, and by 1610 only one dwelling remained on the site, which in 1823 was levelled to create a new wharf. At that time the lower parts of three chambers all about 9m long by about 6m wide were exposed.

The surviving range of the Franciscan Friary at Shrewsbury

SHREWSBURY   Shropshire   *Franciscans*   SU 495121   To SW of English Bridge

In 1245 Henry III ordered the sheriff and the bailiffs of the town to provide a suitable site for a church and house of Franciscan friars. Later that year he donated fifty cart-loads of lime for the construction of stone buildings, and in 1246 permitted the friars to make a gateway through the adjoining town wall. In 1267 they were allowed to widen the gateway to take carts. Richard Pride is said to have built the friars' church, which was of stone, although the provincial minister William of Nottingham ordered that the dormitory should be mud-walled so as to not be too ostentatious.

The precinct occupied three or four acres and lay close to the English bridge on land outside the town wall which was prone to flooding. In August 1420 there was water eight feet deep within the church. The previous year friar John Randolph had ended up in the Tower of London together with Queen Joan, widow of Henry IV, who was ac-cused of witchcraft. He had been Joan's confessor and held in safe keeping some of her possessions. In 1463 the elderly friar Richard FitzJohn was granted a lifetime use of a chamber with a fireplace and garden within the precinct.

In 1525 the Bishop of Hereford licensed Warden William Duffield to preach within his diocese, an indulgence of forty days being granted to all who heard him preach. This warden had the decayed buildings repaired, obtaining funds from the townsfolk, and in 1533 he was made a suffragen of the Bishop of St Asaph. The friary was said to have been in good order when surrendered to the Bishop of Dover in August 1538.

On the riverbank there survives an early 16th century sandstone range thought to have contained the refectory on the south side of the cloister with cellars below it. It was much altered later on to create tenements and re-roofed to provide attic bedrooms above, but retains an original buttress and doorway, plus several windows, including one of three lights with intersecting tracery. A timber-framed range extending west of it was demolished as recently as 1967-9. It had an unheated upper room which could have been a dormitory. The inventory of 1538 also mentions an upper and lower vestry, a kitchen, hall, and a chamber (probably that used by the warden).

SOUTHAMPTON   Hampshire   *Franciscans*   SU 420110   At south end of town

The friary founded c1233-4 was demol-ished on the order of the provincial minis-ter in 1236 because the site was deemed unsuitable. A new stone church was un-der construction in 1280-7 and the chap-ter house and dormitory were completed in 1291. A new water supply was donat-ed in 1290 although it was 1304 before it was connected up to the friary. In 1499 Henry VII changed this friary into a house of the Observant Franciscans. The Friary Gate of 1373 in the town wall still exists. Footings of the closely buttressed choir of the church were revealed in 1980. It appears to have had a porch at the NW corner. Traces of an earlier church were found to the south of it.

The Franciscan Friary at Shrewsbury

STAFFORD   Staffordshire *Augustinians*   SJ 920238   Beyond north end of town

In 1344 Ralph, Lord Stafford founded a friary in Forebridge, a suburb south of the town and some way east of the old castle that Ralph rebuilt in stone about that time. The five acre site was provided with water from a well donated by Ralph's brother-in-law Humphrey de Hastings, Archdeacon of Coventry. The friary was visited by Henry IV just after his victory over the Percies near Shrewsbury in 1403. The Stafford family had their monuments moved here when the priory at Stone was suppressed in 1537, but the friary was surrendered in the following year and stone from it was soon being sold off. The re-erected 14th century arcade in the parish church at Bradley was amongst the 42 cart-loads of stone taken there from the friary in 1542. When surrendered the friary had just minimal and mostly well-worn furnishings including four sets of vestments, two organs, a few books, and one large and one small bell in the tower.

STAFFORD   Staffordshire *Franciscans*   SJ 924228   Beyond south end of town

The Franciscans were established in the town under patronage by the Stafford family by 1274, when the Bishop of Lichfield granted 20 days' indulgence to all those who visited the friary church on certain days and said the Lord's Prayer and a Hail Mary for the king. In 1306 Henry Grucok was proposing to grant the friars more land for their buildings. The friary was surrendered to the Bishop of Dover in 1538 and the buildings were sold to James Leveson, who also took custody of the bells. The lead from the roofs was sold separately and fetched £45. Other items were a statue of St Catherine, a pair of portable organs, four alabaster tables and some old books. By 1610 a house called Grey Friars stood on the site, which lay east of the road to Stone, but this building, which may have contained parts of the friary, was demolished in 1644 to give the Parliamentary forces occupying the town a clear field of fire from the town walls.

STAMFORD   Lincolnshire *Augustinians*   TF 025069   At west end of town centre

In 1342-3 Edward III and the Bishop of Lincoln allowed a house for twelve Austin friars to be established here by Robert de Wodehouse, Archdeacon of Richmond, who was buried in the choir of the church early in 1345. Part of the site, which eventually covered eight acres, had been previously used by the Friars of the Sack, four of whom were fed at the expense of Edward I in 1300. Another part was handed over in 1372 by the Gilbertines of Sempringham. Prior Richard Warnar and five other friars surrendered the house to Dr John London in October 1538. The church was well leaded on the roofs and Dr London sold the glass immediately to prevent it being stolen.

STAMFORD   Lincolnshire *Carmelites*   TF 035074   At east end of town centre

The Carmelites were settled here by 1268, when Henry III gave them six oaks towards work on their church. The royal arms appeared over one of the gates and the house was used by royalty when journeying to and from the north. When a provincial chapter was held here in 1300 Edward I donated £10 towards the costs of the meeting and one of the Stamford friars, William Ludlington, was made provincial prior. Other chapters were held here in 1319 and 1444, and there appear to have been 26 friars in 1314. The friars were allowed in 1317 and 1336 to acquire considerable amounts of extra adjoining land to the north. The precinct seems to have been nearly a mile in circumference and the church was a fine building with a steeple and a full set of lead roofs. Prior John Kyrtun and six other friars surrendered the house to Dr John London in October 1538. A proposal for it to become part of a royal lodging was soon abandoned.

STAMFORD   Lincolnshire *Dominicans*   TF 036073   At east end of town centre

The Dominicans must have arrived in Stamford in the 1230s and occupied a ten acre site near the water-gate, with grounds extending down to the river. Henry III gave them many gifts, such as ten oaks in 1244 towards building a refectory, 15 marks later that year towards building a conduit to bring in water from across the River Welland, and three days' food supplied for a provincial chapter in 1247. Edward I donated ten marks towards another provincial chapter here in 1276, and in 1293 he donated three oaks towards making choir stalls, whilst the late Queen Eleanor had recently left them 100s. There were about forty friars here during that period. In 1310 Bishop Dalderby licensed the dedication of the newly rebuilt church. In September 1320 Edward II donated £15 towards the expenses of another provincial chapter here. The 38 friars fed at the king's expense when he passed through Stamford in 1324 gave him 60 pears from their orchards in return. Edward III spent the Easter of 1332 in the friary and paid 50 marks compensation for damage done by the royal household. The king stayed here again in 1335 and gave £15 towards a provincial chapter in 1340. Another royal grant towards a chapter held here in 1370 was not in fact paid until 1374.

Friar Henry of Aldwinkle managed to escape from imprisonment for a carnal sin. The Dominican master-general sent him off to study theology at Cologne and in 1398 ordered that his offence was never to be mentioned again. He was made chaplain and confessor of a nearby nunnery in 1399. The will of Sir Hugh le Despencer dated 1400 makes provision for the lengthening of the family chapel adjoining the friary church and for a monument to him and his wife and his parents to be set up within it. Two towns-men were charged with an attack upon two of the friars in 1416. Prior William Stafford and eight other friars surrendered the friary in October 1538 to Dr London, who sold the glass and brewing vessels and noted the church had a good set of lead roofs.

STAMFORD   Lincolnshire *Franciscans*   TF 036 073   At east end of town centre

Beside a road junction a small ashlar-faced 14th century gatehouse with blank image niches on the upper parts of its buttresses still survives of this house. The friary exist-ed as early as January 1230 when Henry III granted fuel to the friars. The king donated timber to make choir stalls in 1235, and 100s towards a provincial chapter held here in 1239. At another provincial chapter here ten years later the Franciscans formerly welcomed the Augustinian friars to England. The studium or college for the Franciscan friaries in the custody of Oxford was at Stamford in 1337, probably in conjunction with an abortive attempt to establish a university in the town. The townsfolk prevented the friars from obtaining an extra 7 acres of land beside their precinct in 1365.

In 1385 Richard II's mother Joan, widow of the Black Prince, was buried next to her first husband Thomas Holland, Earl of Kent in a chapel adjoining the friary church, in which was the tomb of Blanche, daughter and heiress of Henry, Earl of Lancaster. In 1402 one of the friars was accused of opposition to Henry IV, and in 1424 friar William Russell had the audacity to preach that a member of the clergy could lie with a woman without committing sin.

In May 1520 Henry VIII donated £10 towards a provincial chapter held here. When the houses of the Observant Franciscan houses were suppressed in 1536 three of them were sent here as effectual prisoners. Warden John Schewyn and nine other friars surrendered the friary to Dr London in October 1538. Most of the buildings had been dismantled by 1541 when the 11 acre site was granted to the Duke of Suffolk.

Franciscan Friary gatehouse at Stamford

Timber-framed gatehouse of the Dominican friary at Sudbury

SUDBURY   Suffolk   *Dominicans*   TL 871411   On south side of the town centre

Baldwin de Shipling and his wife Chabil were buried in the choir of the church of the Dominican friary which they had founded on a five acre site sometime before 1247, when Henry III gave the friars six marks. In 1299 the chaplain Robert de Pettemer was allowed to give the friars an adjacent strip of land and in 1352 the Archbishop of Canterbury's father Nigel gave the friars another eight and half acres of land. Archbishop Simon Chertsey and his brother John donated a spring and permission to connect it to the friary, although local opposition to the laying of the conduit across the lands of others delayed this project for nearly five years. When Edward I visited nearby Waddington in 1296 he donated 30s to provide thirty friars here with three days' food. Royal sponsorship of £15 on each occasion was provided for provincial chapters held here in 1316 and 1368.

In 1530 Prior Geoffrey Jullys and the other friars granted the use of a house to the west of their church to John Hodgkin D.D., who had taught theology at the friary before becoming provincial prior. Being initially regarded at court with suspicion he was replaced in this office by John Hilsey after the establishment of the royal supremacy over the church in 1534. However he wrote a submissive letter to Thomas Cromwell and regained both the provincial's office and the use of the lodging at Sudbury near the end of 1536, and a year later was made one of several new suffragan bishops, with the title Bishop of Bedford. Although the friary was surrendered in 1538 and by October 1539 had been granted to Thomas Eden, a clerk of the king's council and his wife Griselda, Hodgkin got his lease registered in the Court of Augmentation and resided in the lodging in the friary precinct until given the vicarage of Saffron Walden in Essex in 1541. He married during Edward VI's reign but had to temporarily repudiate his wife and express penitance to obtain preferment from Cardinal Pole during Queen Mary's reign.

THELSFORD Warwickshire *Trinitarians* SP 274582 7km south of Warwick

A farm to the east of the Warwick to Wellesbourne road lies on or near to the site of a monastic house founded c1200 by Henry de Barford and originally occupied by canons of the short-lived Order of Holy Sepulchre. By 1214, when it was further endowed by Sir William Lucy of Charlecote with another 13 acres, the house seems to have passed to Trinitarian friars who were charged by Sir William with running a hospital and hostel for pilgrims. Further lands were later donated by the de Lucy family and the friars were allowed to enclose a road running between their church dedicated to St Redegund and their house. In 1394 there was a particularly large gift of 46 acres of land from Sir William Lucy, Roger Strange and John, Vicar of Wellesbourne.

In 1312 the deans of Warwick and Hampton were ordered by the Bishop of Worcester to publicly absolve the minister and brethren at Thelsford who had been excommunicated on a charge of fabricating letters purporting to be from Pope Clement. In 1411 the Pope granted plenary remission to the minister, friars and sisters here. The sisters may have been lay-women rather than nuns. Sir Edmund Lucy in his will dated 1498 asked to be buried to the north side of his mother Margaret in the Lady Chapel of the friary church. He left money for masses for his soul and those of his relatives for six years. His widow Joan was buried beside him in 1514. The friary was valued in 1535 as having revenues worth almost £25. In October 1538 Prior Edmund David and three other friars surrendered the house to Dr London. The Lucy family failed in their bid to recover the site and lands, which were granted to the Cheneys. The friars' house was then said to be ruinous and the church was small and had been left incomplete.

THETFORD Norfolk *Dominicans* TL 866831 On the south side of the town

In 1335 the site of the former cathedral, where ruins of an incomplete Early Norman church and cloister had stood for centuries, was handed over by Henry, Earl of Lancaster to the Dominicans for a new friary. The earl made the very unusual stipulation that the priors of the house were always to be nominated by the lords of Thetford, although the original founder's deed was lost in a fire here in 1410. The earl of Surrey gave the friars a long narrow strip of adjoining land in 1338. Pope Boniface IX in 1393 granted a two year indulgence to all those that visited the friary on feast days and contributed to its maintenance. In 1424 the friars allowed the Benedictine prior and monks of Bury St Edmonds Abbey to use a chamber in the friary precinct when on business as patrons of the parish church and administrators of the lands of the nunnery of St George.

Prior Richard Cley and five other friars signed the undated deed of surrender in 1538. Overgrown lengths of walling with tall blank arches and one tall, narrow arch of the central tower survive of the church in the grounds of a school beside London Road.

Remains of the Dominican friary church at Thetford

THETFORD   Norfolk   *Augustinian*   TL 876828   At SE end of town centre

John of Gaunt, Duke of Lancaster, founded this small house for six friars c1387. He endowed it with 36 acres of land in Thetford and Barsham and the profits from the fair of St John the Baptist. The friary was placed as far as possible from the Dominican friary, thus honouring Richard II's undertaking to the Dominicans in November 1386 that no other houses of friars would be built near their premises. The duke built the Augustinian friars a church with a cloister and other buildings on the south side and he handed over the old chapel of St John on the west side of the town to serve as the chapel of a leper hospital to be run by the friars. Further land was also donated by Sir Thomas de Morle and others.

In 1408 the friars were allowed to enlarge their church by removing a house that stood between it and the street, and a hermitage presumably for an anchorite was to be built at the west end. A major benefactor during this period was Lady Tuddenham, d1412, who is now commemorated by an urn of 1807 placed in a nearby field after her burial vault was destroyed when the Georgian house called Ford Place was erected at the end of Old Market Street. In September 1538 John Hilsey, Bishop of Rochester found the friary to be in a very poor state and closed it down on the spot, the deed of surrender being signed by prior Nicholas Pratt and two other friars. The friary then lacked any contents of value and had no lead on the roofs.

TICKHILL   Yorkshire   *Augustinian*   SK 585928   At the SW corner of the town

This friary is thought to have been founded in the 1260s by John Clarel, a canon of Southwell Minster. Edward I allowed the friars in 1276 to inclose a track between their church and land held by William Clarel, and in 1279 they were given four royal oaks towards work on their church. There appear to have been 18 friars in 1300 when Edward gave them all a day's food. A similar donation by Edward III in 1335 was for 24 friars. The parish church contains a fine tomb chest with effigies of Sir Richard Fitz-William and his wife Lady Lucy Neville, daughter of John, Marquess of Montague which came from the friary church. In the friary church was also buried the heiress Elizabeth Clarel and several other members of the Scrope and Fitz-William families, one of the latter being killed at Flodden in 1513. Prior Richard Robinson and seven other friars surrendered their house to Sir George Lawson in November 1538. The church was covered in lead, there were two bells in the tower, and the furnishings included a clock and two old portable organs. The place appears to have been later known as Clarel Hall.

What appear to be the east and ranges of the buildings still survive in a much altered condition as a private house, with a later block now connecting them. The west range has a tall window with Y-tracery of c1300 and an original chimney-breast, the mullioned and transomed windows being of the period after the suppression. Inside it is an octagonal pier with an embattled fleuron capital carrying a pair of four-centred arches with an angel in the spandrel. The other range has buttresses at the south end, and an old arch on the outside of the west wall. There is another arch in the garden which is clearly 13th century as it has dog-tooth ornamentation.

TRURO   Cornwall   *Dominicans*   SW 824451   On north side of the town centre

The friary existed by the mid 13th century and lay between Kenwyn Street and the river. The Bishop of Exeter in 1355 appointed friar Roger Tyrel to be a confessor for non-English speaking Cornish locals. Ralph Keskmer was a benefactor in 1463.

WALSINGHAM   Norfolk   *Franciscans*   TF 933366   At the SW edge of the village

Despite considerable opposition from the canons of the nearby Augustinian priory this friary intended for twelve friars was founded in 1347 by Elizabeth de Burgh, Countess of Clare. The friars were allowed to enclose a road below their house in 1351 and in 1440 they were given considerable extra lands by Richard, Duke of York. The friary was surrendered to Richard Ingworth, Bishop of Dover late in 1538.

The private grounds in which the ruins lie also include a house and are not open to the public, although a good view of the SE corner of the buildings can be seen from a roadside gateway. Slightly more has survived of the domestic buildings here than of any other English Franciscan house. A lane separated the main cloister from the church, which had an aisled nave five bays long separated by a walking place from an aisleless choir of which low walls remain. Much still stands of the west range containing the guest rooms, which was also separated from the cloister by a lane. The now rather ruinous upper rooms were presumably intended for Lady Elizabeth to use herself. The dormitory lay over the southern half of the eastern alley of the cloister, with the chapter house north of it. The refectory lay above both the southern alley of the main cloister and the northern alley of a smaller southern cloister which remains fairly complete except for the outer wall on the south side, where a staircase interupts the regular pattern of three-light windows between buttresses facing the garth. These windows are later medieval although with its northern alley underlying the refectory the southern cloister is clearly part of the original 14th century layout. The kitchen lies west of this second cloister, with the modern house close to it, whilst the reredorter serving the dormitory seems to have extended along much of the eastern side of the second cloister. Along this cloister's southern side probably once lay the infirmary hall.

The west range of the Franciscan friary at Walsingham

Ruins of the Franciscan Friary at Walsingham from the SE

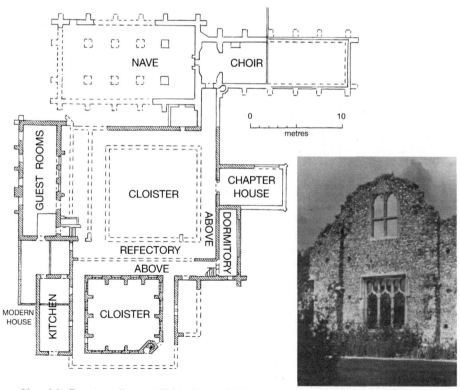

Plan of the Franciscan Friary at Walsingham at 1: 800 scale

Franciscan Friary at Walsingham

The south range of the Franciscan friary at Ware, showing the cloister alley windows

WARE   Hertfordshire   *Franciscans*   TL 353143   At the SW corner of the town

This friary was founded in 1338 by Thomas, second Lord Wake of Liddell. The friars were forbidden by the Pope in 1395 to beg in places that were normally frequented by friars from Cambridge. In 1430 the recently deposed Provincial Minister Roger Dewe went into exile here. The friary was surrendered by five friars to the Bishop of Dover in June 1538. Parts of the buildings were converted into a house by the Byrch family, who lived here until 1628. It passed through several other families until purchased in 1685 by the Hadsley family, two of whom, successively sheriffs of Hertfordshire in the 1740s, did further work to modernise the building. Still further work was done for the Gosselin family in the mid 19th century. Now known as Ware Priory, the building is now used by the local council as offices and function rooms.

Little is known about the church on the north side of the cloister or the eastern range, but most of the south range survives, along with the southern half of the west range and another original wing projecting west of it. This wing probably contained guest rooms and has a small original quatrefoil-shaped window. The chief remaining medieval features are several buttresses and the three-light windows which once lighted (several are now blocked) the south and west alleys of the cloister which formed part of the lowest storey of the south and west ranges. In the south range the dividing wall between the alley and the rooms under the refectory has now been removed. Footings of another building were exposed by the fall of a tree in the grounds in 1990.

WARRINGTON   Cheshire   *Augustinians*   SJ 607879   South side of town centre

By 1308 Augustinian friars seem to have taken over an older hospital. Chantries were founded in the church by Sir Thomas Dutton in 1379 and Sir John Bold in 1422 and probably lay in the large fully aisled north transept four bays long. There was a tower between the nave and choir, neither of which had aisles. After being surrendered in 1539 the friary was sold to Thomas Holcroft. An office block of now lies on the site of the church and its cloister. There was a large outer court.

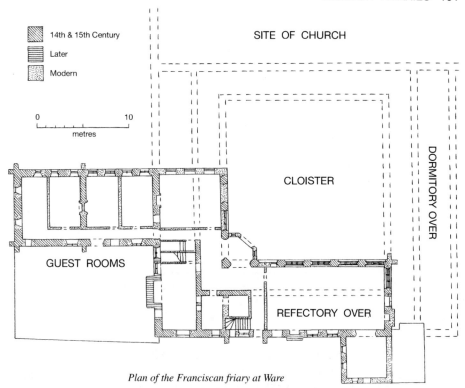

14th & 15th Century

Later

Modern

0   10
metres

SITE OF CHURCH

CLOISTER

DORMITORY OVER

GUEST ROOMS

REFECTORY OVER

Plan of the Franciscan friary at Ware

WARWICK   Warwickshire   *Dominicans*   SP 278647   Outside west walls of town

Ralph Boteler of Wem was a great benefactor to this friary, the church of which was under construction in 1263. There were 30 friars here in 1329. More land was given to them in 1344 and 1361. Their possessions were valued at £5 in 1535. Prior Thomas Norman and seven friars surrendered the friary in 1538 to Dr London, who described the buildings as ruinous and having lead only on the gutters and the steeple. He immediately defaced the windows and the dormitory cubicles. It appears that one of the roofs was taken off to a building then under construction at nearby Warwick castle.

WINCHELSEA   Sussex   *Dominicans*   TQ 903173   To the SW of the present town

Despite Edward I having promised that only the Franciscans would have a house within the new town of Winchelsea replacing the old one destroyed by a great storm in 1287, the Dominicans were eventually granted a twelve acre site at the far end of the town by the southern or New Gate. They found themselves isolated from the townsfolk as no domestic houses were ever built at this end, and in 1339 were allowed to transfer to a six acre plot below the town. However this site was liable to inundation and in 1358 Edward III allowed the friars to move a second time to a one acre plot in the centre of the town near St Giles Church, with permission to acquire five adjoining messuages. In 1402 the prior was arrested for treason against Henry IV. The Bishop of Dover found the buildings in a ruinous state when he arrived to take possession in 1538. A ruined building with trapdoors into crypts is thought to be part of the east end of the church.

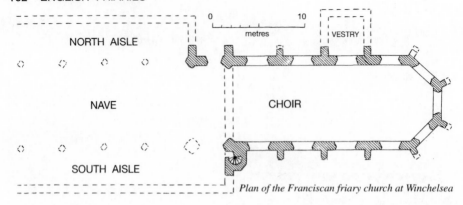

NORTH AISLE

VESTRY

NAVE

CHOIR

SOUTH AISLE

Plan of the Franciscan friary church at Winchelsea

WINCHELSEA   Sussex   *Franciscans*   TQ 175901   Beyond SE corner of the town

Lying in the large private grounds of a mansion near the town is the 14th century choir of the friary. It has four full bays and then a polygonal east apse. There is a wide arch at the west end where a fragment with a staircase turret remains of the east end of the south aisle of the nave. The large windows have all lost their tracery and the buttresses have lost their quoins. A squint remains from a sacristy on the north. The Franciscans were established in this area before 1253, when Richard, Bishop of Chichester left them a bequest, and there is a mention of land in the Pevensey salt-marshes being leased to them in 1263, but little is known about their subsequent history.

WINCHESTER   Hampshire   *Augustinians*   SU 480289   To SE of the city centre

This friary was founded in the 1270s or 80s and was given more land by Geoffrey Spiring in 1302 and by the bishop in 1328. The bishop was ordered by the pope in 1343 to allow the friars to move to a manse within the walls as the original site outside the south gate was rather exposed. The new site lay opposite the church of St Michael in College Mead. This name recalls the fact that Winchester College eventually acquired the sites of all four of the friaries within the city.

Two views of the Franciscan friary church at Winchelsea

WINCHESTER   Hampshire   *Carmelites*   Location Uncertain

This small house founded in 1276 lay near the Augustinian friary and was deserted when the Bishop of Dover arrived in the city in 1538.

WINCHESTER   Hampshire   *Dominicans*   SU 285293   NE of the cathedral

Peter de Roche brought over a few Dominican friars to his diocese of Winchester in 1225 and attempted to establish them in Portsmouth. This project fell through, probably because of Bishop Peter being away from the diocese until 1230, but the friars were then settled on a two and a half acre site in Winchester near the Eastgate end of the High Street, bounded by Bucket Street on the west and the River Ichen on the east. Henry III gave each of the twenty eight friars here a pair of shoes and four ells of cloth to make a tunic in 1239 and he donated 100s towards the expenses of a provincial chapter here in 1259. Henry III also donated wood for building works and fuel on several occasions, notably ten oaks for completion of the refectory in 1256, and sixteen oaks in 1269-70 for ornamenting and roofing the church, which was dedicated to St Catherine. Edward I also donated timber in 1298 and dead oaks for fuel on several other occasions, There were forty six friars here in 1325, when Edward II gave them alms for a day's food, although the number was down to thirty six when Edward III made a similar gift in 1331. These kings also helped sponsor provincial chapters here in 1315 and 1339 and the friary had a chamber reserved for the use of provincial priors.

The names survive of quite a number of the priors of this friary through the years. Prior James Cosyn adopted some of the most extreme ideas of the early 16th century reformers and got into trouble after preaching a sermon in a local church in 1536 against confessions to priests, the blessing of bread, and the use of holy water. An inventory by the Bishop of Dover, who took the surrender of the friary in 1538 includes a number of vestments, hangings and altar-cloths, two portable organs, three beds with bolsters and the usual list of minor domestic furnishings and utensils.

WINCHESTER   Hampshire   *Franciscans*   Location uncertain

This friary is first mentioned in the will of Richard, Bishop of Chichester in 1253. It was surrendered in the summer of 1538. Little else appears to be known about it except that in 1330 the body of Edmund of Kent which was temporarily buried here after his execution was exhumed later in the year after the regime of Queen Isabella and the Earl of March collapsed, and was then sent to Westminster for permanent burial.

WOODHOUSE   Shropshire   *Augustinians*   SJ 647771   NW of Cleobury Mortimer

This was one of the earliest of the Augustinan friaries in England, and seems to have existed by 1250. The remote location would have appealed to the early ideals of the order, and it was only after the union of the most important groups of friars following the rule of St Augustine that locations in towns to allow both preaching and begging were preferred. Alms here would have been thin on the ground so endowments were necessary, and the friary eventually acquired an estate of fifty acres. The founders may have been the Turbervilles, who were tenants of Gilbert de Clare, Earl of Gloucester, founder of the Augustinan friary at Clare. William Langland, author of Piers Plowman, was either a member of the community or educated here. In 1537 Bishop Rowland Lee arrested the prior for having sold off the furnishings of the house and changed his habit. Four other friars surrendered the house in August 1538. A moat survives but the house within it was rebuilt in the mid 19th century and the old chapel has now gone.

WORCESTER   Worcestershire   *Dominicans*   SO 849551 At north end of city

This friary opened off Broad Street at the north end of the city and was one of the last Dominican houses to be founded in England. It was established in 1347 with William Beauchamp, Lord of Elmley as patron. He was allowed by Edward III to donate more land in 1351 on the understanding that a daily mass was said for the king and his heirs. The friars built a gateway on the extra land but did not have full possession of it as the priors of Great Malvern and St Mary's in Worcester each claimed a part of it. Further land for the enlargement of the friars' garden was donated by Richard II in 1391.

A warrant was issued for the arrest of friar William Shyrburne and the confiscation of his "magical books" in 1431. Sir John Beauchamp's will of 1475 directed that he be buried in a tomb with an alabaster effigy in a new chapel to be added to the north side of the choir. He also left the friars various furnishings and vestments, including two portable organs then in the parish church of Chelsea in Middlesex, and his other bequests included a daily donation of 2d towards the friars' food and 40 marks towards completion of the cloister and repairs to the other buildings. John's widow Margaret also made several bequests in 1487 and arranged for a monument to herself surmounted by a tablet showing the Birth of Christ to be erected in the new chapel. Other notables buried in the church were Richard Wycherley, titular Bishop of Olenus in Greece, and Richard Wolsey, Bishop of Down and Connor in Ulster.

After accepting the surrender of the house from Prior Richard Edwards in August 1538 the Bishop of Dover wrote to Thomas Cromwell saying that he had had difficulty in persuading an anchoress living here to leave and that there was no lead on the buildings, which were decayed. Several of the ten sets of vestments were incomplete and the other furnishings were of little value apart from what was in 'the chambers", where there were five feather beds with bolsters. Two small organs and a large bell and a small bell are also mentioned. Both the Worcester friaries were granted to the city in December 1539, materials from them being intended for the repair of the city walls.

WORCESTER   Worcestershire   *Franciscans*   SO 851547 On the west side of city

The Franciscans seem to have been established here by 1226, when they were joined by Peter de Eport, Rector of Stoke Prior. A more famous recruit here in 1230 was Adam de Marisco. The Worcester friary was the head house of a custody that by the 14th century included the English houses at Coventry, Lichfield, Stafford, Preston, Chester and Llanfaes on Anglesey. In 1231 Henry III ordered the city bailiffs to enlarge a postern to help the friars bring in fuel, but under Albert of Pisa (1236-39) they moved to a nearby site outside the walls. A 16th century house now maintained by the National Trust within the walls retains the name Greyfriars but no actual medieval friary buildings.

Oaks from royal forests for building works were granted in 1257, 1276 and 1282, and a provincial chapter was held here in 1260. William Beauchamp, Earl of Warwick was buried in 1298 in the choir of the church whose construction he had sponsored, and his father had also been buried there in 1268. Bishop Giffard actively supported the Franciscans, and in 1275 they preached in favour of a crusade in churches throughout the diocese. Relations with the monks of the cathedral-priory were less good, causing Archbishop Peckham to intervene in 1290 following a quarrel over the burial place of an important citizen named Henry Poche. Other notable patrons of the friary included the Beauchamps of Powick, and members of the Cokesey and Throckmorton families. In 1485 there is a reference to the friars' dormitory as having recently fallen down. The house was reluctantly surrendered to the Bishop of Dover in August 1538.

WORCESTER   Worcestershire   *Friars of the Sack*   Location Unknown

In March 1272 Henry III granted to these friars a street called Dolday to allow the expansion of their premises. After the 1274 Council of Lyons they were forbidden to take any fresh recruits and must have died out here by the early 14th century.

YARM   North Yorkshire   *Dominicans*   NZ 421126   On the SE side of the town

A house of the 1770s called The Friarage stands on the site of a friary which existed by 1266, when Henry III gave the friars ten oaks from Galtres Forest. The de Brus family were major benefactors, although further lands were given by Sir Marmaduke de Twenge of Danby and a local burgess named John de Aslacby. In 1302 and again in 1304 the prior complained about others putting cows on lands claimed by the friars. In 1291 the Archbishop of York asked the friars here to preach in favour of a crusade in Allerton, Thirsk and Yarm. Royal donations for food were for 30 friars in 1299, for 33 friars in 1319, and for 28 friars in 1335, when a further donation was made for repairing the cloister. The archbishop allowed the Scottish Bishop of Whithorn to dedicate the newly completed church in 1308, but in 1315 he asked the friars to denounce the Scots for devastating the neighbourhood and to stir up the local people to resist them.

Benefactors during the 14th and 15th centuries included the Percy, Latimer, Mowbray and Conyers families and here were buried many of the Hiltons of Hilton and the Meynells of Hilton. In 1520 Friar Clement Guadel was sent here by the master-general to teach in the Grammar School after services. Just before Christmas 1538 the friary was surrendered to William Blytheman by Prior Miles Wilcock, five friars and six novices, a remarkably high number of the latter. The prior was given 20s and the others 54s from the sale of the friary's goods for £108. The friars had held here ten acres of lands and eight cottages yielding annual rents of £3 12s 8d.

YORK   Yorkshire   *Augustinians*   SE 601520   Near Lendal Bridge, north of centre

Friars from Tickhill are said to have established themselves here on the bank of the Ouse and in 1272 were given a writ of protection by Henry III. Edward I donated them six oaks in 1292. Royal gifts of food indicate 35 friars in 1300 and similar numbers in the 1330s, although there were only 26 in 1320, probably because some had been sent off to found a new house at Hull. Friar Richard de Wetwang was one of those summoned in 1311 to a provincial council at York to take measures against the Templars. More land was obtained in the 1350s and 70s and in 1361 the archbishop contributed 5s towards a provincial chapter held here. In the British Museum in London, the College of Arms and two Oxford colleges there still survive a few books from the friary library, from which a catalogue dated September 1372 still survives listing as many as 646 books and manuscripts, half of which had once belonged to Master John Erghome.

In 1411 Pope John XXIII encouraged the giving of alms to a recently founded guild chapel of St Catherine in the friary church. Amongst those buried in the church were the Neville brothers Sir Humphrey and Charles executed at York in 1469. The king's brother Richard, Duke of Gloucester often stayed at the friary in the 1470s and the Earl of Northumberland paid £4 6s. 8d for lodging within it several times during 1522-23. Here in 1493 the abbot of St Mary's and the mayor met to discuss a dispute between the weavers and the cordwainers of the city. Prior John Aske seems to have escaped unpunished for supporting the Pilgrimage of Grace in 1535. Ten friars and four novices surrendered the friary in November 1538, when an inventory mentions the church as having two bells and forty fother of lead on the roof.

YORK   Yorkshire   *Dominicans*   SE 598515   SE of the station, west of city centre

At the instigation of Henry III the Dominicans in 1227 took over the chapel of St Mary Magdalene and a plot of land behind it extending to the river. The friars may however have been temporarily housed in Goodramgate beforehand. In 1236 Prior Alan sent a man to prison for having "bad opinions on the articles of faith". Henry III warned the prior that this action was beyond his jurisdiction but the king acknowledged that there were many non-believers in the district and ordered the sheriff to arrest and imprison them at the prior's mandate. Several gifts of timber from royal forests were made during this period and some more land was granted by the king in 1268. The York house was the head of one of the four visitations into which the English province was divided and hosted provincial chapters under royal sponsorship in 1235, 1246, 1256, 1275, 1289, 1306 and 1329. Under it were the houses at Berwick, Bamburgh, Beverley, Carlisle, Lancaster, Lincoln, Newcastle-upon-Tyne, Pontefract, Scarborough and Yarm.

In 1275 servants of the Archbishop of York were attacked and beaten when they tried to rescue from the pressure of the crowd some boys about to be confirmed in the friars' church. The king gave the friars a vacant plot of land near the river but their attempt a few years later to obtain another piece of land east of the friary failed because it was needed for military musterings and the occasional erection of siege engines. Royal alms given for food indicate 60 friars here in 1307, 48 in 1312, 54 in 1318, and about 50 during the 1330s. Archbishop Greenfield in 1314 licensed for service a new chapel in or beside the friary church which had been built by Sir Henry Percy, and he exhorted all Dominican preachers, and especially the prior of Yarm, to denounce the Scottish raids and to encourage the local people to resist them. One of the three John de Wycliffes ordained in the friary church in 1350-51 must have been the famous reformer. In 1358 the friars tried to recover a young friar called William de Newton, who had been seized and taken off by his family.

Richard II ordered those who had broken down a wall in the friary precinct in the riots of 1381 to repair it, and in 1385 he attended here the funeral and temporary burial of Sir Ralph Stafford, who had been murdered by Sir John Holland. Shortly afterwards Sir Brian Stapleton gave to the friars a relic of the right hand of St Mary Magdalene. On account of the great value and importance of this he was regarded as the second founder and was buried in the church. His son married into the Aldeburgh family, who were also important benefactors. Other notables buried in the church were Robert de Neville of Raby in 1282, Humphrey de Bohun, Earl of Hereford, John Mowbray and Roger Clifford, who were all killed in the battle of Boroughbridge in 1322, Catherine, Lady Greystoke, c1413, and several members of the Stangeways family.

In 1456 the archbishop proclaimed an indulgence of forty days to those willing to help rebuild the friary cloister and its buildings after a fire which had destroyed them, complete with thirty-four cells and a lecture-room, plus all the books, chalices, vestments and furnishings. In 1537 Prior John Pickering was hanged at Tyburn for his part in organising the Pilgrimage of Grace in 1536. He wrote many letters in support of the rebellion and also a protest song which was popular amongst the rebels. The priory was surrendered in November 1538 to Sir George Lawson and William Blithman by the new prior, six friars and four novices. The valuables included a silver hand which presumably housed what remained of the hand of St Mary Magdalene, and the church had two bells and 34 fother of lead on its roof. A proposal at that time that the Dominican friary buildings be renovated and extended using materials from other friaries to form a mansion and council house for The Council of the North was never carried out.

YORK   Yorkshire   *Franciscans*   SE 604513   West of Clifford's Tower (castle keep)

This house seems to have been founded c1230 and was the head of a custody which eventually included houses at Beverley, Boston, Doncaster, Grimsby, Lincoln and Scarborough. Henry III donated as many as sixty oaks from royal forests in 1236-37 and the house expanded rapidly, necessitating a change of site in 1243 to a location between the castle ditch and the River Ouse. In 1268 the king allowed the friars to make a preaching enclosure within a moated outwork of the castle provided that the land was available for defence in time of war. The friars were asked by Archbishop Romanus in 1291 to preach in Howden, Pocklington, Selby and York in favour of a new crusade. During this period Henry de Lacy, Earl of Lincoln was a major benefactor and the friars built a stone wall along the bank of the Ouse. It diverted the force of the river onto the opposite bank, and in 1305 the king was obliged to order the walling in of that bank also, the costs being borne from funds available for walling the city.

In 1303 the archbishop allowed the dedication of the newly completed church and cemetery. There were as many as 52 friars here in 1299, but in 1300 there were just 43. Royal alms for food given in 1311, 1319 and 1320 suggests numbers of 36 to 40, with a rise to 50 by 1335 and a drop again to about 45 in the late 1330s. Edward II resided in the friary instead of the adjacent castle in 1319-20, public business being conducted in the chapter-house. Some of the meetings of the parliament held at York in 1322 seem to have been held in the friary. When the teenage Edward III stayed at York for several weeks in 1327 to counter the raids by the Scots he and his mother Isabella, then Queen Regent, stayed in the Franciscan friary, each having separate households. According to Froissart the queen staged a feast for sixty of her ladies in the friars dormitory, but the proceedings were disrupted by a street fight just outside between the York citizens and her unpopular Hainault mercenaries. There was another royal visit in 1335, when the king ordered the repair of a wall and well beside the kitchen doorway and gave 100s in compensation for damages. In 1359 Edward III ordered that the rights of sanctuary were to be respected, following an incident in which city officials had broken into the precinct. In 1380 Richard II took the friars under his special protection and ordered that the river and adjacent lanes should not be defiled with carcases and rubbish, since he was inclined to lodge in the friary precinct when visiting York.

A provincial council was held here in 1361 and in 1399 Boniface IX conferred special privileges on Friar Henry Bilton, ordering that he was to be well treated by his brother friars at this house. In the 1420s Friar William de Melton persuaded the authorities to curb the activities of the many prostitutes in the city and also introduced reforms into the mystery play performed on Corpus Christi Day. Later in the century several Franciscans were admitted as members of the Corpus Christi Guild of York. In a service staged here in 1397 the archbishop ordained four friars from each of the Franciscan and Augustinian houses, plus five Carmelites and six Dominicans. At another service held here in 1501 clerical orders were conferred on as many as seven Franciscans, five Augustinians, two Carmelites and just one Dominican.

Some of outlying lands given to the friary formed the endowment of the Roecliff Mass, a chantry in the friary church founded in 1495 by Brian Roecliff of Cowthorpe under the terms of his will. He and his son Sir John and his brother Thomas were all buried in the friary church. Sir John's will provided for a tomb depicting him under the Trinity but this was never executed for lack of assets. In November 1528 Warden William Vavasour S.T.P., fifteen other friars and five novices surrendered the house to Sir George Lawson. The church had two bells and was covered with 60 fother of lead.

YORK   Yorkshire   *Carmelites*   SE 606518   To the east of Fossgate, SE of centre

The Carmelites originally had their house in Bootham, near the Horsefair. Donations from Henry III included oaks from royal forests towards building a church in 1253 and 1255, an extra piece of land in 1258, and two marks towards a provincial chapter in 1260. They later moved to a site bounded by Stonebow Lane on the north, Fossgate on the east, the Foss on the south and Mersk Lane on the west which was donated in 1295 by William de Vesci. His successors the Percies were later major benefactors. Edward I donated eight oaks towards a new church on the second site in 1300 and the new cemetery was consecrated in 1304. There appear to have been about 25 friars at this time. In 1314 the friars allowed Robert of Pickering, Dean of York to take over their original site to found a chapel and hospital of St Mary. That same year Edward II handed over some more land donated by Geoffrey de St Quintin and allowed the friars use a boat on the king's stew of the foss and to build a quay to be served by this boat, which was engaged in bringing in building materials. The York house was head of one of the four distinctions into which the Carmelite province of England was divided.

   In March 1358 Edward III granted protection to the teenage son of John de Thornton, who had joined the Carmelites when a child but had thrown off his habit and was being persecuted by the friars, who regarded the lad as apostate. In 1374 there is a record of the killing (probably accidental) of Friar John Harold by Friar John Wy. Several lawsuits by priors are known from this period, relating to debts, the taking of soil by a potter, and the collapse of badly built oven. Prior Simon Clerkson and nine friars and three novices surrendered the friary in November 1538 to Sir George Lawson, when the church had two bells and was estimated to have 20 fother of lead roofing.

YORK   Yorkshire   *Friars of the Sack*   Location Unknown

This house seems to have been founded c1260. Two of its members were ordained priests in 1274. Edward I gave alms for two friars here in 1300 but after they died their property reverted to the crown.

OTHER POSSIBLE REFERENCES TO COMMUNITIES OF FRIARS

DURHAM   - In 1237 when the see was vacant Henry III had a small donation made to Franciscans in the city out of its revenues.

GILLINGHAM   - In 1267 Henry III gave the Dominicans twelve oaks to repair what was probably just a chapel beside his royal palace here in Dorset.

JARROW   - Dominican friars here were provided with food by Edward III in 1329, but they may actually have been based at Yarm.

LYME REGIS   - In 1325 there was an attempt to establish Carmelite friars here.

MAIDSTONE   - John Atte was allowed to donate two messuages and six acres to the Franciscans but in spite of this no friary ever appears to have been established here.

ROMNEY   - Henry granted money for clothes for members of a short-lived Franciscan friary here at Romney in Kent in 1241.

SHERBORNE   - In 1343 there was an attempt to establish Augustinian friars here.

WOTTON-UNDER-EDGE - In 1349 Edward III allowed lands worth £10 per annum to be donated to some friars here in southern Gloucestershire.

GLOSSARY OF TERMS

Aisle	-	A passage beside part of a church.
Anchorite	-	A hermit or religious recluse.
Archdeacon	-	A church dignitary ranking next below a bishop.
Ashlar	-	Masonry of large blocks cut to even faces and square edges.
Black Friar	-	A member of a Dominican friary, usually dressed in a black habit.
Chancel	-	The eastern member of a church reserved for priests and choristers.
Chapter House	-	A room where monks, priests or friars met daily to conduct business.
Choir	-	A part of a monastic church containing stalls for monks, nuns or friars.
Clerestory	-	An upper storey pierced by windows lighting the floor below.
Cloister Alley	-	A walkway along one side of a cloister.
Cloister Garth	-	The central court or garden of a cloister, surrounded by four alleys.
Cruciform Church	-	Cross-shaped church with transepts forming the arms of the cross.
Cusps	-	Projecting points between the foils of a foiled Gothic arch.
Custodian	-	The head of a grouping of friaries known as a custody.
D.D.	-	An abbreviation of the degree of Doctor of Divinity.
Grey Friar	-	A member of a Franciscan friary, usually dressed in a grey habit.
Jamb	-	The side of a window, doorway or open opening.
Lancet	-	A long and comparatively narrow window, usually pointed headed.
Lavatorium	-	A lavatory or washing place, usually next to the refectory entrance.
Mendicant	-	Begging, or living solely on alms.
Messuage	-	A dwelling house with outbuildings and lands.
Nave	-	The part of a church in which the lay congregation stood or sat.
Norman	-	A division of English Romanesque architecture dating c1066-1200.
Ogee-headed window	-	Topped by a curve which is partly convex and partly concave.
Oratory	-	A small chapel either standing alone or forming part of a large building.
Oriel	-	A bay window projecting on corbelling.
Piscina	-	A stone basin used for rinsing out holy vessels after a mass.
Prior	-	The head person of a priory or friary or the deputy head of an abbey.
Provincial Chapter	-	A gathering of representatives of houses of any monastic order.
Quoin	-	A cut stone used to form part of a corner.
Refectory	-	The main dining room of a monastic house.
Reredorter	-	The toilet of a monastic house, usually at the far end of a dormitory.
Reticulation	-	Window tracery with a net-like appearance.
Rood Screen	-	A screen with a crucifix mounted on it between a nave and a chancel.
Sacristy	-	A part of a church were vestments and sacred vessels were kept.
Sedilia	-	Seats for clergy (usually three in the south wall of a chancel or choir.
Sexton	-	A person who looks after a church and churchyard.
S.T.P	-	An abbreviation for a Professor of Sacred Theology.
Suffragan	-	A bishop appointed to assist a diocesan bishop.
Tie-Beam	-	A beam connecting the slopes of a roof, usually at wall-plate height.
Tierceron Vault	-	A vault designed with both major and minor ribs.
Transom	-	A horizontal member dividing upper and lower lights in a window.
Wall-Plate	-	Horizontal beam laid on top of a wall to form part of a roof.
Warden	-	The head of a Franciscan or Trinitarian friary or a hospital.
Walking Place	-	A cross passage between the nave and the choir of a friary church.
Warming Room	-	The only room in a friary where ordinary friars had access to a fireplace.
White Friar	-	A member of a Carmelite friary, usually dressed in a white habit.
Wind Braces	-	Braces connecting and helping to stabilise the rafters of a roof.

HOUSES OF FRANCISCAN & DOMINICAN NUNS

BRUISYARD   Suffolk   *Franciscan Nuns*   TM 333662   NW of Saxmundham

In 1354 a chantry with four chaplains and a warden was moved out to Rokehall in the parish of Bruisyard from where it had originally been founded in 1340 within the nunnery church of Campsey. In 1366 its premises were handed over to the Franciscan Sisters of St Clare, often known as Poor Clares on account of their continual poverty. St Clare had "renounced the world" in 1212 and was soon joined by other women, for whom a rule based on that of St Francis was approved by the pope in 1219. The order is wide-spread throughout the world today but only had three houses in medieval England. The sisters obtained adjacent lands and control over the local parish church by an exchange of lands with the nuns of Campsey in 1385. In 1535 the nunnery was reckoned to have an annual value of £56 and it paid £60 to avoid being suppressed in that year, when it had a parlour, several chambers, a buttery, kitchen, bakehouse and brewhouse, all said to be poorly furnished. It was finally surrendered to the king's commissioners in February 1539 by Abbess Mary Page. The house on the site known as Bruisyard Hall is mostly a three storey brick building of 1610 with a central porch but the western part contains an older room with a heavily beamed ceiling and some medieval walling with one original arch. Some old walling also survives further south.

DENNY   Cambridgeshire   *Franciscan Nuns*   TL 495684   10km NE of Cambridge

Denny was a Benedictine cell of Ely from 1159 to 1169, and then passed to the Knights Templar, who completed the nave of the small cruciform church in a shorter form than originally intended, with a two bay arcade into a south aisle. The building nearby to the SW was probably a house of a priest. The Templars used Denny as a hospital for older members of that order until they were suppressed in 1308. It then passed to the Knights Hospitaller but they appear to have made no use of it and left it to decay.

Edward III granted Denny to Mary de St Pol, widow of Aymer de Valance, Earl of Pembroke. She converted the crossing and transepts of the original mid 12th century church into a residence for herself and then handed most of the rest of the site over to Poor Clares or Franciscan nuns originally established at Waterbeach in 1294 (where foundations have been found by excavation). For them the countess built a new aisled church in place of the original choir, and a cloister to its north with a dormitory and a refectory, whilst the original nave and aisle and priest's house became a guest house. After the countess died in 1377 the abbess is assumed to have taken over her rooms. These parts later became a farmhouse and have survived roofed and intact, but with considerable alterations, and some of the upper rooms now have no floor-boards. The arches of the original crossing and arcade remain, some parts of the inserted blocking walls having been cut back to reveal the well-preserved capitals of the responds.

After the nunnery was suppressed in 1539 Abbess Elizabeth Throckmorton retired with two or three other nuns to continue to live an enclosed life at her original family home of Coughton Court in Warwickshire until she died in 1547. Meanwhile Denny went to Pembroke College at Cambridge. Tenant farmers lived here until the 1960s, and since 1997 the abbey site has formed a part of a farmland museum. A tiled floor was revealed in 1987 within the much-altered nuns' refectory on the north side of the cloister which had long served as a barn. Several windows and traces of the reader's pulpit also remain. All the other monastic buildings have gone, the only relic of the nuns' church being a remarkably tall respond of its north arcade adjoining the crossing and transepts of the earlier church converted into a farmhouse.

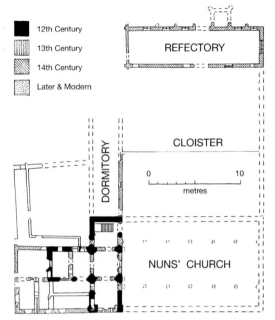

12th Century
13th Century
14th Century
Later & Modern

REFECTORY

CLOISTER

0   10
metres

DORMITORY

NUNS' CHURCH

Plan of Denny Abbey at 1:800 scale

Denny, junction of old and new churches

LONDON   *Franciscan Nuns*   TQ 337811   To north of Tower of London

Excavations near St Clare Street, Tower Hamlets in 1984 revealed one wall of the church of the Franciscan nuns or Poor Clares or Minoresses founded in 1293. Parts of the west range with two doorways have been found in a nearby warehouse. The church of the Holy Trinity was rebuilt in 1706 and destroyed by bombing in 1940.

The 12th century church at Denny converted into a house for the abbess

DARTFORD   Kent   *Dominican Nuns*   TQ 540746   To NW of town centre

Edward I's widow Eleanor of Castile promoted the idea of a Dominican nunnery in England and Edward II attempted to establish one at Guildford. Eventually it was the vintner William Clapitus and Edward III that founded the only medieval Dominican nunnery in England at Dartford in 1349. The vintner provided two messuages and ten acres of land and the king provided most of the endowments of lands and appropriated churches, plus a lot of the money for constructing the buildings. The priory was under the control of the prior of King's Langley and its considerable endowments yielding an income of £361 in 1535 were intended to help support the King's Langley friars. At that time the prioress stated to Thomas Cromwell that the high steward or seneschal of the estates was by long-standing custom a member of the king's council.

With royal officials under instruction to impress all available craftsmen, work on the buildings progressed quickly. It appears that 40 nuns were originally envisaged. In practice a prioress and three other nuns from Brabant moved into the priory in 1356 and another ten soon joined, whilst there were also six friars, the senior of whom bore the title of president. In 1358 Edward III gave 200 marks towards work on the church, and another 100 marks for lead to roof the church and other buildings. Richard II was also generous enough to the priory to be regarded as a second founder. In 1384 there is a mention of the infirmary chapel. In the early 15th century the nuns tried to shake themselves free of being subservient to King's Langley but were unsuccessful.

Nuns' refectory at Denny, now converted to a barn

By 1481 the provincial of the order normally appointed the president with the consent of the nuns, whilst the prioress chose the confessor for the nuns. During that period Edward IV's daughter Bridget was placed here as a ten year old girl. She took the veil in 1490 and lived until 1517. The prioress was usually from a noble family, the nunnery being noted as a place of education for nuns and gentlewomen not destined to be nuns. The priory survived until as late as April 1539. It was retained in royal hands and a courtyard house built in the southern half of the precinct to accommodate royalty when in transit from London to Dover. One range with blocked four-centred arches and a latrine projection still remains on a site in the middle of the Dartford Iron Works entered from Hythe Road. Just one arch and parts of the precinct wall in Kingsfield Terrace remain of the medieval buildings but the site was excavated in 1913 by Sir Alfred Clapham and found to have a normal monastic layout. The choir of the church dedicated to St Mary and St Margaret contained the tomb of Catherine, widow of Sir Maurice Berkeley, d1526.

Queen Mary reinstated the nuns in 1557 but Elizabeth I soon closed the priory down again down, sending the community of two priests, a prioress and four choir nuns, plus four lay sisters and a young unprofessed girl in exile over to Antwerp. Queen Elizabeth herself stayed in her father's new house in 1559, and made another visit in 1573.